In the
Neatest Manner

Williamsburg Decorative Arts Series

Graham Hood, *Editor*

British Delft at Williamsburg
by John C. Austin

Chelsea Porcelain at Williamsburg
by John C. Austin

English and Oriental Carpets at Williamsburg
by Mildred B. Lanier

English Silver at Williamsburg
by John D. Davis

Furnishing Williamsburg's Historic Buildings
by Jan Kirsten Gilliam and
Betty Crowe Leviner

The Governor's Palace in Williamsburg: A Cultural Study
by Graham Hood

New England Furniture at Williamsburg
by Barry A. Greenlaw

Rebellion and Reconciliation: Satirical Prints on the Revolution at Williamsburg
by Joan D. Dolmetsch

Southern Furniture 1680–1830: The Colonial Williamsburg Collection
by Ronald L. Hurst and Jonathan Prown

The Williamsburg Collection of Antique Furnishings

Wallace Gallery Decorative Arts Publications

Eighteenth-Century Clothing at Williamsburg
by Linda Baumgarten

English Slip-Decorated Earthenware at Williamsburg
by Leslie B. Grigsby

In the Neatest Manner: The Making of the Virginia Sampler Tradition
by Kimberly Smith Ivey

Silver at Williamsburg: Drinking Vessels
by John A. Hyman

Tools: Working Wood in Eighteenth-Century America
by James M. Gaynor and Nancy L. Hagedorn

Worcester Porcelain in the Colonial Williamsburg Collection
by Samuel M. Clarke

In the Neatest Manner: The Making of the Virginia Sampler Tradition

Kimberly Smith Ivey

CURIOUS WORKS PRESS
&
THE COLONIAL WILLIAMSBURG FOUNDATION

In the Neatest Manner:
The Making of the Virginia Sampler Tradition

This book was prepared in conjunction with the exhibit *Virginia Samplers: Young Ladies and Their Needle Wisdom*, October 31, 1997, to September 8, 1998, at the DeWitt Wallace Gallery, The Colonial Williamsburg Foundation, Williamsburg, Va.

Printed and bound in the United States of America

Published by Curious Works Press, 107 RR 620 South, Austin, Tex. 78734
and The Colonial Williamsburg Foundation, Williamsburg, Va.

00 99 98 97 5 4 3 2 1

ISBN 0-0633331-8-6 for Curious Works Press
ISBN 0-87935-202-7 for the Colonial Williamsburg Foundation

All items illustrated are owned by the Colonial Williamsburg Foundation unless otherwise specified.
AARFAC denotes the Abby Aldrich Rockefeller Folk Art Center, Williamsburg, Va.
DAR denotes the Daughters of the American Revolution Museum, Washington, D.C.
MESDA denotes the Museum of Early Southern Decorative Arts, Winston-Salem, N.C.

All measurements are expressed by width followed by height.
Stitches listed in the legends are in alphabetical order. Whenever possible, stitch terminology follows the glossary section of Susan Burrows Swan's revised edition of *Plain & Fancy: American Women and Their Needlework, 1650–1850* (see bibliography).
In order to preserve their original tone, all excerpts from primary sources retain their archaic spellings, capitalization, punctuation, and the use of underlining.

Colonial Williamsburg photography by Hans E. Lorenz and Craig McDougal.
Additional photographs supplied by the British Museum, London, England; The Carter House, Franklin, Tenn.; Kathleen Epstein, Austin, Tex.; Iberian Publishing Company, Athens, Ga.; Maryland Historical Society, Baltimore, Md.; Daughters of the American Revolution Museum, Washington, D.C.; Museum of Early Southern Decorative Arts, Winston-Salem, N.C.; Smithsonian Institution, National Museum of American History, Washington, D.C.; Skinner, Inc., Boston, Mass.

Front and back covers: obverse and reverse sides of sampler by Sarah Bruce Butt, age 13, dated June 18, 1811. See figure 97.
Inside front and back covers: *Williamsburg Female Academy*, ca. 1845. See figure 88.

Graphics by Betty Demarest

For my mother, a Virginia Lady
who taught me needle
wisdom and much more —
and for Virginia girls everywhere,
past, present, and future.

DONORS AND LENDERS TO THE EXHIBIT

Donors

Antique Collectors' Guild
Louise Barbour
Sarah Barbour
Mary Wrenn Cofer Ballard
Nancy Chappelear Baird
Mrs. John Lewis David
Leslie Carr Miller Haas
Janet Cook Howard
Jeannine's Sampler Seminar
Ernest LoNano
Mrs. Edwin H. Phelps
Mrs. Lewis F. Philhower
Sumpter T. Priddy III
Mrs. and Mrs. Philip R. Roper, Jr.
Betty Skarohlid
Joan Rozier Stephens
Bettyanne B. Twigg
Mr. and Mrs. Howard Via
Grace Hartshorn Westerfield
Williamsburg Rose and Thistle Chapter of the Embroiderers' Guild of America

Lenders: Private Collectors

Anne Biscoe Johnson Behm
Martha Wren Briggs
Ellen Taylor Donnelly
Elizabeth Adams Lane
Roddy Moore
Mrs. Adeline B. Ransone
Charles and Elizabeth Umstott
Alma B. White
Esther C. White

Lenders: Museums

Arlington House, United States National Park Service, Arlington, Va.
Association for the Preservation of Virginia Antiquities, John Marshall House, Richmond, Va.
Baltimore Museum of Art, Baltimore, Md.
Children's Museum of Indianapolis, Indianapolis, Ind.
Clarke County Historical Association, Berryville, Va.
Jamestown-Yorktown Educational Trust, Williamsburg, Va.
Loudoun Museum, Leesburg, Va.
The Lyceum, Alexandria's History Museum, Alexandria, Va.
Lynchburg Museum System, Lynchburg, Va.
Museum of Early Southern Decorative Arts, Winston-Salem, N.C.
Sully Foundation, Ltd., through the Fairfax County Park Authority, Fairfax, Va.
Valentine Museum, Richmond, Va.
Virginia Historical Society, Richmond, Va.

CONTENTS

FOREWORD

COLONIAL WILLIAMSBURG'S magnificent collections reflect and represent an entire cross section of Anglo-American, eighteenth-century society. They range from great objects that would be featured in any art museum's galleries to humbler items that are more characteristic of a historical society's holdings. Inevitably, the expensive, virtuoso products reserved for richer consumers have survived intact more frequently than the everyday items of less affluent people, which were so often discarded when worn or broken, or adapted for different purposes and used until worn out.

So it is welcome to find a group of objects the compass of which is almost entirely drawn around a relatively restricted subsection of that society—females under the age of about twelve, whose family circumstances enabled them to receive special schooling. It is a surprise and a pleasure to see these products of young girls' hands and minds—and it is an extra pleasure to see a young curator, through perseverance and discernment, segregate a group of these products characteristic of one particular location and a fairly restricted time frame.

This book is yet another product of American scholars' continuing search to identify regional groups of material products. But it is an unusual grouping that is catalogued herein, since it shows overt exercises in the formulation of a moral life, and in both intellectual and manual training.

It is a great pleasure to welcome this book in conjunction with an exhibition on the same topic in the DeWitt Wallace Gallery at Colonial Williamsburg from October 31, 1997, to September 8, 1998. Both the book and the exhibition are the products of a young curator's dedication and unremitting hard work—and deep-rooted pleasure, which we hope will reflect on those who read these pages and who contemplate the objects in the exhibition.

Colonial Williamsburg is very grateful to Kathleen Epstein for her role in the production of the book and to generous lenders and the DeWitt Wallace Fund for Colonial Williamsburg, created by the founder of *Reader's Digest*, for making the exhibition possible.

Graham Hood
Vice President, Collections and Museums
Carlisle H. Humelsine Curator

PREFACE

THE COLONIAL WILLIAMSBURG Foundation began collecting samplers and needlework almost from the beginning of its history. In 1930 the newly formed foundation purchased its first sampler, a small British piece worked on a worsted ground (fig. 27). During the 1950s and '60s English and American samplers were added to the collection, mostly for display in the historic buildings. In 1971 an anonymous gift of thirty-seven samplers, many formerly owned by Gertrude Whiting and Mrs. DeWitt Clinton Cohen, tremendously enhanced the collection. Surprisingly, it was not until 1978 that Colonial Williamsburg purchased its first Virginia sampler (fig. 94). Four years later, with only three Virginia samplers in the collection, Linda Baumgarten, Curator of Textiles, launched a commitment, supported by Graham Hood, Vice President, Collections and Museums, and Carlisle H. Humelsine Curator, to seek out and actively collect and document samplers and other embroideries worked by Virginia girls. I was extremely fortunate to be given this opportunity and challenge.

Since that time I feel as if I have been putting together the pieces of a huge puzzle—a puzzle that even today is missing some of its most important pieces. Why are there so few colonial Virginia samplers? Did Virginia girls work samplers in the seventeenth century, and if so, were they as sophisticated as those worked in England? Who were these girls and teachers and what was their relationship to one another (figs. 127-131)? Where is Sarah Hornsby's Williamsburg sampler, the only reference to which is so tantalizingly described by Ethel Stanwood Bolton's and Eva Johnston Coe's classic 1921 reference work, *American Samplers*? And, most importantly, how do these Virginia samplers illuminate the lives of the makers and teachers?

Complicating the research are several problems peculiar to Virginia. For example, many counties are "burned counties," meaning that county records taken to Richmond for safe keeping during the War Between the States were lost in fire. One such county is James City, which borders the colonial capital of Williamsburg. Second, old Virginia families intermarried continuously and first names were reused often within the same generation. Thus, determining who's who can be a formidable task. Unlike New England needlework from the same time period, many Virginia samplers closely resemble their English and Scottish counterparts. The fragile condition of some embroideries also adds to the difficulty of studying them.

Despite these and other obstacles, an overwhelming body of raw data on Virginia samplers and embroideries has been collected. In recent years, more than two hundred Virginia samplers have been discovered and documented. Once thought to be nonexistent, Virginia samplers have assumed a new and integral place in the study of American needlework and female education. Although so little is currently known about so many of the young makers of these remarkable embroideries—apart from their surviving samplers—Virginia girls are now receiving recognition for their technical expertise and needle wisdom through a major exhibit and this catalog, which accompanies it. However, the exhibit and catalog are not all inclusive. With each question answered a new one is raised; thus, the research is ongoing and warrants future exhibitions and publications. Information on Virginia samplers is always welcomed.

ACKNOWLEDGMENTS

THE EXHIBIT *VIRGINIA Samplers: Young Ladies and Their Needle Wisdom* and this catalog would not have become a reality without the contributions of a number of individuals and institutions who gladly gave of their time, skill, and knowledge. Some of the greatest rewards in this project have been the interesting and warm people I have met, the old family stories I have heard, and the collections I have seen. I am indebted to many for their gracious hospitality in allowing me into their homes and for their willingness to lend and give. A list of donors and lenders to the exhibit and catalog can be found opposite the table of contents.

I extend my sincerest thanks to my colleagues, past and present, at the Colonial Williamsburg Foundation who have been instrumental in this project: Liz Ackert, Suzanne Coffman, Dywana Saunders Confroys, Rebecca Fass, Loreen Finkelstein, Pat Gibbs, Margaret Gill, Jan Gilliam, Gail Greve, Rick Hadley, Graham Hood, Ron Hurst, Robert Jones, Mildred Lanier, Hans Lorenz, Barbara Luck, Jane Mackley, Craig McDougal, April Metz, Roberta Null-Hair, Phyllis Putnam, Anne Schone, Susan Shames, Tracey Stecklein, and John Watson.

I am especially indebted to Linda R. Baumgarten, Curator of Textiles, and Carol Harrison, volunteer emeritus. Linda, who offered me my first opportunity to work with this collection, not only shared her extensive knowledge of textiles and source materials, but allowed me the freedom to grow. Many of the references found in the text of this catalog were first brought to my attention by her. Carol shared her knowledge of stitches and was always there for the many road trips, the double-checking of information, the pulling and restoring of objects, and never-failing words and deeds of support.

Colleen Callahan at the Valentine Museum gave me unrestricted access to their large and important collection of Virginia embroideries. William Rasmussen at the Virginia Historical Society was also generous with his time and collection. Much of my research was based on the earlier work of the Museum of Early Southern Decorative Arts. I am especially indebted to Jennifer Bean, Johanna Metzgar Brown, and Martha Rowe of the MESDA staff for their recent assistance. Other scholars and researchers who contributed their expertise are: Gloria S. Allen, Ann Fassuacht, Betty Whiting Flemming, Deborah Kraak, Glee Krueger, Sumpter T. Priddy, Betty Ring, Sue Studebaker, and Susan Swan.

When Kathy Epstein graciously offered to publish this catalog jointly with Colonial Williamsburg, I auspiciously gained not only a publisher, but an editor deeply immersed in women's history and needlework. She guided me through this project with her good cheer, abounding energy, and incredible perceptiveness. Her suggestions and reflections were of enormous assistance as I formulated thoughts and conclusions. I am indeed grateful to Kathy for her editorial and technical assistance.

My friends and family have been wonderfully supportive of me and my Virginia girls. I am especially appreciative of the many times Judi Howard watched my young son play outside while I worked inside at what he calls the "puter." On many occasions my husband, Gordon, rescued transcripts that had "crashed and burned" on the computer due to my unexplained incompatibility with the machine. For this and his faith in me, which gave me the courage to attempt this project, I am unequivocally thankful.

PROLOGUE

FEMALE EDUCATION

A YOUNG LADY may excel in speaking French and Italian; may repeat a few passages from the volume of extracts; play like a professor, and sing like a syren; have her dressing-room decorated with her own drawing tables, stands, flower pots, screens and cabinets; nay, she may dance like Semphronia herself, and yet we shall insist, that she may have been very badly educated. I am far from meaning to set no value whatever on any or all of these qualifications; they are all of them elegant, and many of them tend to the perfecting of a polite education. These things, in their measure and degree may be done; but there are others which should not be left undone. Many things are becoming, but "one thing is needful." Besides, as the world seems to be fully apprised of the value of whatever tends to embellish life, there is less occasion here to insist on its importance. But, though a well-bred young lady may lawfully learn most of the fashionable arts, yet, let me ask, does it seem to be the true end of education, to make women of fashion dancers, singers, players, painters, actresses, sculptors, gilders, varnishers, engravers, and embroiderers? Most men are commonly destined to some profession, and their minds are, consequently, turned each to its respective object. Would it not be strange if they were called out to exercise their profession, or set up their trade, with only a little general knowledge of the trades and professions of all other men, and without any previous definite application to their own peculiar calling? The profession of ladies, to which the bent of their instruction should be turned, is that of daughters, wives, mothers, and mistresses of families. They should be, therefore, trained with a view to these several conditions, and be furnished with ideas, and principles, and qualifications, and habits, ready to be applied and appropriated, as occasion may demand, to each of these respective situations. Though the arts, which merely embellish life, must claim admiration, when a man of sense comes to marry, it is a companion whom he wants, and not an artist. It is not merely a creature who can paint and play, and sing, and draw, and dress, and dance; it is a being who can comfort and counsel him; one who can reason, and reflect, and feel, and judge, and discourse, and discriminate; one who can assist him in his affairs, lighten his cares, soothe his sorrows, purify his joys, strength his principles, and educate his children. Such is the woman who is fit for a wife, a mother, and a mistress of a family.

Mrs. Ware, "Female Education,"
The Lady's Book, vol. 2 (December 1830), p. 309.

Figure 1. Sampler by Lilias Blair McPhail, age nine, ca. 1828; "Norfolk," Virginia. The needlework teacher responsible for this style has yet to be identified.

Silk on linen ground of 29 x 30 threads per in.; 22 3/4 in. x 16 3/4 in. Stitches: back, couching, cross, outline, straight.

Photograph courtesy The Baltimore Museum of Art; Gift of Mrs. Francis White, from the Collection of Mrs. Miles White, Jr.

ONE

"To promote the happiness of the little circle"

LIKE OTHER FORMS of material culture, samplers are products of a particular society and thus reflect attitudes, expectations, and changes within that society. Samplers are also works of art that not only please modern eyes, but tell us what was considered aesthetically pleasing in the past. More importantly, these examples of plain and decorative needlework illuminate the lives of people often overlooked in written history: the girls and women who lived during the seventeenth, eighteenth, and nineteenth centuries.

Samplers help us understand their makers' world, often giving us details of their creators' names, ages, families, and locations (fig. 2). The materials used to create them indicate the kinds of embroidery supplies available in local stores. The stitches illustrate some of the practical skills thought necessary for a female to acquire in order to be the successful mistress of a household. Enduring sampler styles testify to the influence of needlework teachers. The embroidered religious and moral verses forcibly remind us of the high expectations parents had for their daughters. Samplers, then, are essential guides to a better understanding of the societies in which these girls and women lived and of how these societies differed from place to place and over time. Much of the information revealed by samplers can be grouped into four important themes: life passages, the female compass, moments in time, and "respectfully presented."

LIFE PASSAGES

During the second half of the eighteenth and early nineteenth centuries, a transformation of per-

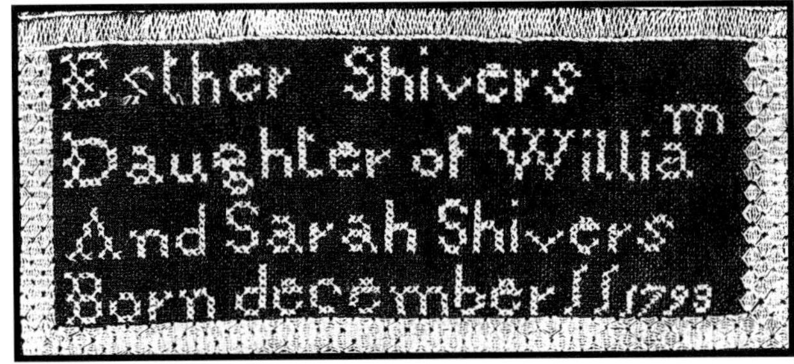

Figure 2. Detail of sampler by Esther Shivers, dated 1808; Nansemond County, Virginia. The entire sampler is illustrated in figure 96.
The Loudoun Museum, Bequest of Joan Stephens

sonal values and relationships took place within the family unit. The father-dominated family of the seventeenth century and colonial era, with its emphasis on paternal control, obedience, and restraint of emotions, slowly evolved into a more openly affectionate and private family environment in which children became the center of attention (fig. 3).[1] Different role expectations for individual family members developed as parents paid more attention to each child's disposition and traditional concerns with family lineage and land became less important.[2] During this time, the happiness and well-being found in family life provided the emotional and economic supports that earlier had been supplied by the larger community and public sphere. These changes resulted in a more openly affectionate American family, firmly rooted in the rights of the individual.[3]

We see these changes reflected in the material culture and the writings of the time. For example, in an 1804 letter to her mother in Belgium, Rosalie Stier Calvert, wife of wealthy Maryland planter George Calvert, wrote, "Each day I realize more and more that happiness is only to be found in one's family."[4] Fifteen years later, in 1819, Alexis de Tocqueville noted in his *Democracy in America*:

Figure 3. Black and white mezzotint engraving entitled *The Happy Family*, from a painting by Jean Baptiste Greuze; dated April 5, 1773; printed in London.
1968-441

Individualism is a mature and calm feeling, which disposes each member of the community to sever himself from the mass of his fellows and to draw apart with his family and friends, so that after he has thus formed a little circle of his own he willingly leaves society at large to itself.[5]

A group of three samplers worked in Norfolk, Virginia, in the second decade of the nineteenth century clearly resonates with this belief (fig. 1).[6] At the top of each sampler, an observation was carefully executed in cross stitch: "The daughter who loves her home will take a lively interest in all of its concerns and be solicitous to promote the happiness of the little circle of which she forms a part." This adage not only reminded the young stitchers that a woman's place during this period was in her home but it also reinforced the importance of home and family life as seen through nineteenth-century eyes.

One type of sampler, referred to today as a family record, or register, sampler, reflects the changes

Figure 4. Sampler attributed to Martha Ann Waring, ca. 1824; attributed to Essex County, Virginia. Martha (born 1812; died September 20, 1881) was the second child of William Lowry Waring and Elizabeth Chilton Hudnell of Essex County. She married Robert Wright of Popular Grove, Virginia, on December 11, 1828. They had four children (*Essex County Marriage Register, 1804–1921*, reel 103; *Register of Births, 1856–1916*, reel 103; and *Register of Deaths, 1856–1916*, reel 103).

The upper portion of this sampler consists of a poem dedicated to Mrs. Elizabeth Waring, Martha's mother, who died April 2, 1814, at the age of twenty-five, and a family record listing the second marriage of her father in that same year to Mary Banks. The poem reads "Let sorrow for her early doom / No more in silence sigh / For hope which points beyond the tomb / Bids every tear be dry / When we devote our youth to god / Tis pleasing in his eyes / A flower that's offer'd in the bud / Is no vain sacrifice." The needlework teacher responsible for Martha's sampler was probably Mary Elliot Tompkins, whose name, along with sets of initials that may represent Mary's family members, were also stitched on the sampler.

Silk on linen ground of 26 x 29 threads per in.; 16 15/16 in. x 17 7/16 in. Stitches: cross, hem, marking cross, and queen's.
G1986-126,A; Gift of Mrs. John Lewis David

Figure 5. This daguerreotype of Martha Ann Waring in the form of a brooch descended in the Waring family along with the sampler in figure 4.
1 1/8 in. x 1 7/8 in.
G1986-127; Gift of Mrs. John Lewis David

that took place in the family. This style seems to have been especially popular with Virginia girls, probably because of the overriding importance Southerners placed on the family.[7] These samplers also give the modern viewer a wealth of genealogical information (figs. 4 and 5). The stitched charts feature birth, marriage, and death dates for the needleworker's parents and siblings, and occasionally other family members or friends. By the second decade of the nineteenth century, especially in Virginia, such records often became embroidered memorials for deceased family members or commemoratives of other life passages (fig. 6).

Figure 6. Sampler by Margaret Kerr, dated January 26, 1828; attributed to Augusta County, Virginia. Margaret's sampler commemorates two life passages: the death of her brother, Bailey Kerr, who died in 1823, and Margaret's own marriage to Elijah Hogshead in 1827 (*Augusta County Marriage Records, 1813–1845*). Incorporated into the sampler are human hair (presumably Bailey's own) and a paper silhouette of her brother.

Silk on linen ground of 40 x 40 threads per in.; 9 7/8 in. x 12 3/4 in. Stitches: couching, cross.
1989-112

THE FEMALE COMPASS

During the seventeenth, eighteenth, and early nineteenth centuries, religious discussions and personal spiritual reflection were essential aspects of everyday life and education for girls and young ladies. Moral lessons played a dominant role in that education (fig. 7). Emphasis was placed not only on a woman's role in the home as a successful housekeeper, but also as an obedient wife and virtuous mother (fig. 8). Keeping within prescribed boundaries of decency, care, and prudence was often equated with wealth and happiness.

Figure 7. *Diligence & Dissipation*, hand-colored etching with line engraving by Thomas Gaugain and Hellyer; London, dated May 1, 1796. This is one plate from a set of ten depicting a moral tale of two sisters, "Diligence" and "Dissipation," who choose opposite paths in life. Dissipation's is an existence of reckless indolence that ends in ruin and disgrace. In contrast, Diligence is shown kneeling in prayer, her sampler hanging on the door as a symbol of her virtue and industry. She is rewarded for her pure life by a prosperous marriage.
1974-94,4

Figure 8. *Keep within Compass*, hand-colored line and mezzotint engraving, printed for and sold by Carington Bowles; dated August 16, 1785; London. The full title of the print advises its viewers: "KEEP WITHIN COMPASS AND YOU SHALL BE SURE TO AVOID MANY TROUBLES WHICH OTHERS ENDURE. PRUDENCE PRODUCETH ESTEEM." For eighteenth-century women, keeping within prescribed boundaries—being prudent—was equated with wealth and happiness. The last stanza of the poem reminds women that they will be surrounded with folly and woes should they step outside the boundaries of decency and care.
1958-629,1

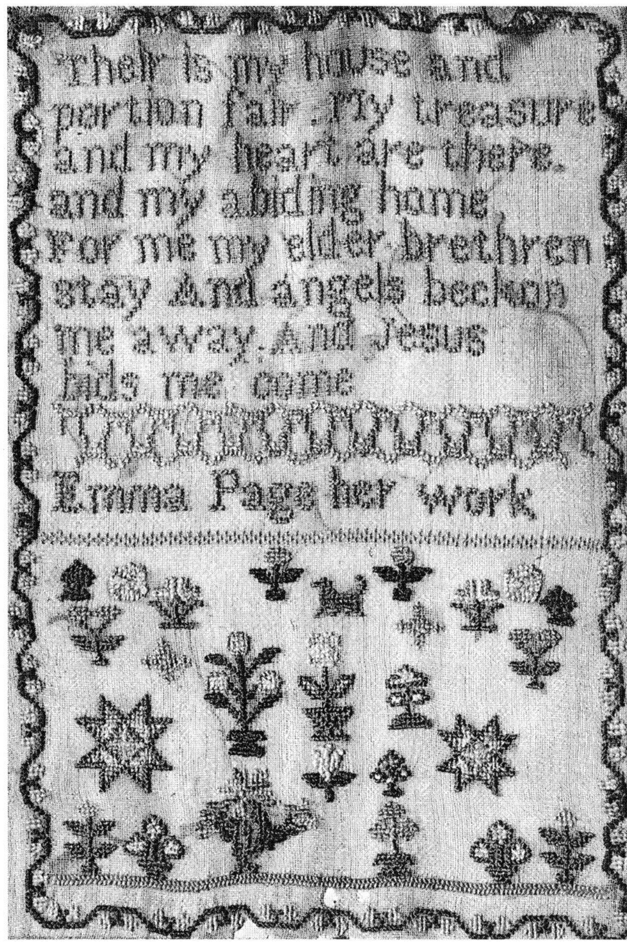

Figure 9. Sampler by Emma Page, ca. 1840; attributed to Clarke County, Virginia. Emma was born at her family's estate, Pagebrook, in 1833. She married Philip Nelson of Nelson County and had two children before "angels beckoned her away" in 1860 at the early age of twenty-seven (Richard C. M. Page, *Genealogy of the Page Family in Virginia*, pp. 147–149). Emma's diminutive sampler includes the following religious verse: "Their is my house and / portion fair. My treasure / and my heart are there. / and my abiding home. / For me my elder brethren / stay And angels beckon / me away. And Jesus / bids me come."

Silk on cotton ground of 80 x 82 threads per in.; 3 3/4 in. x 5 1/2 in. Stitches: cross, herringbone.
1981-162

It is no surprise then that a religious or pious verse was an integral element of the sampler, appearing on the earliest known Virginia sampler, which is dated 1742 (fig. 73). These embroidered expressions conveyed society's high moral expectations for its daughters by instructing and advising the young sampler maker on how she should live her life in preparation for death (figs. 9 and 10).

Sources for these inscriptions were numerous and varied. Many verses were taken from the popular published writings of men such as Alexander Pope and Isaac Watts. Reverend Watts, in particular, was a favored English religious author, best known for his children's hymns and verses.[8] Published almanacs were another major source for poems. Still others may have been composed or adapted by the needlework teacher or perhaps even the needleworker herself.

Figure 10. Detail of sampler by Sarah E. Randolph, age ten, dated August 1833; "Warwick," Virginia. The sampler is inscribed with this reverent stanza: "Tis religion must supply Solid comfort when we die." Warwick was a town on the south side of the James River below Richmond in Chesterfield County, Virginia. It was also the name of a plantation in that same area, owned by Brett and Henry Randolph. Although other members of the Randolph family are recorded in various Chesterfield County legal documents of the period, no mention of Sarah E. Randolph has been found (Benjamin Weisiger, *Chesterfield County, Virginia Deeds 1756–64*; and Frances Earle Lutz, *Chesterfield, An Old Virginia County*, p. 112).

Silk on linen ground of 27 x 28 threads per in.; 17 in. x 17 1/2 in. Stitches: cross, double cross, eyelet, four-sided, queen's.
1992-166

At least two hundred different verses have been recorded from Virginia samplers.[9] Some of these same poems appear on samplers made elsewhere in schools along the East Coast, as well as in Canada and Great Britain.[10] Sometime in the 1830s,

Figure 11. Sampler by Catharine S. Camp, age twelve, 1830–1840; the Carolinas, Georgia, or Alabama. In addition to stitching the most popular sampler verse, which begins "Jesus permit they gracious name to stand," Catharine also worked the following words of advice: "All is the gift of industry / whate[v]er exalts embellishes / and renders life delightful" and "Count that day lost / whose low descending sun / Views from thy hand / no worthy action done." Bolton and Coe noted that this latter verse appears on a sampler dated 1795 and was published in *Staniford's Art of Reading*, 3rd edition, Boston, in 1803 (*American Samplers*, p. 336).

Silk and crinkled silk on linen ground of 27 x 29 threads per in.; 17 1/2 in. x 17 3/8 in. Stitches: back, cross, hem, queen's, satin, split.

1990-196

Catharine S. Camp worked her version of the most popular verse of the eighteenth and nineteenth centuries (fig. 11):

> Jesus permit thy gracious name to stand
> As the first efforts of an infant hand
> And while her fingers o'er this canvass move
> Engage her tender heart to seek thy love
> And write thy name thyself upon her heart.[11]

Moments in Time

By capturing moments in history, samplers can transport the modern viewer back in time. These events can be as simple as the birth date of a sampler maker. Or the recorded incident can involve the community or society at large. In fact, a few rare samplers celebrate public events, memorialize disasters, and protest such social and political institutions as slavery and war (fig. 64).

One exceptional schoolgirl endeavor, by Sally Clark Washington, commemorates the tragedy of the Richmond Theatre fire, which consumed at least seventy-two people, many of them distinguished citizens of Richmond, on the night of December 26, 1811 (fig. 12). In addition to prints, published broadsides, poems, and newspaper articles highlighted the calamity (fig. 13). So notable was the event that discussions of the fire can be found in news articles of the early twentieth century. It also inspired numerous sermons on the moral dangers of theatregoing, many of which were printed and distributed widely.[12] In Sally's sampler, the commemorative poem and the building representing the theatre were taken from a broadside published after the fire.[13] Instead of windows filled with shooting flames, Sally stitched trees behind the building, in keeping with typical sampler design (fig. 12A).

Anne Maria Clarke's sampler, "An Invitation to La Fayette," provides a wonderful illustration of the

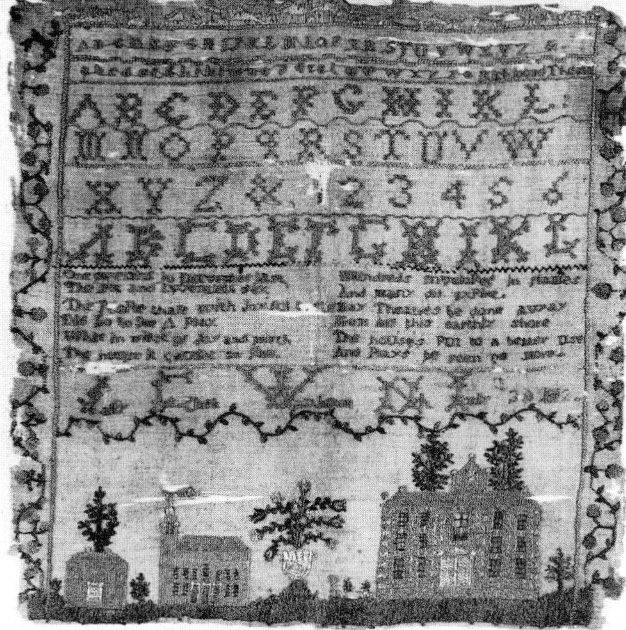

Figure 12. Sampler by Sally Clark Washington, dated December 26, 1811. Sally finished her sampler seven months after the tragedy of the Richmond Theatre fire. From the placement of the words, it is not clear if the maker's name is Sally Clark or Sally Clark Washington. If the former, Washington might refer to the place where the sampler was worked. Stylistically, this sampler has characteristics relating to embroideries of both Washington City and Richmond schools. The unusual Scottish alphabet, seen both mid-way down the sampler and in the signature line, may eventually assist in determining the provenance.

Silk and crinkled silk on linen ground, 19 in. square. Stitches: chain, couching, cross, eyelet, herringbone, outline, satin, stem, straight.
Valentine Museum, 81.119

Figure 12A. Detail of the house in Sally Clark Washington's sampler.

Figure 13. "The BURNING of the THEATRE in RICHMOND, VIRGINIA, on the Night of the 26th December 1811, *By which awful Calamity upwards of* ONE HUNDRED *of its most valuable Citizens suddenly lost their lives, and many others, were much injured.*" Hand-colored aquatint, dated February 25, 1818; Philadelphia.
1995-89

Figure 14. Sampler by Anne Maria Clarke, age twelve, dated January 30, 182[?]. What little is known about Anne's life has been gleaned painstakingly from records. She was probably the daughter of Archibald and Maria Mauzey Clarke, whose marriage was recorded as taking place on October 21, 1807, in Henrico County, Virginia, adjacent to Richmond. Sometime between 1841 and 1844 Anne became the second wife of George Knox Crutchfield, a sign and house painter of Henrico County. Together they had three children, one of whom died at age three. Anne died in 1851 at the age of thirty-nine and is buried at Shockoe Hill Cemetery in Richmond. I am indebted to Susan Adler for this information; see her research report, "Anne Maria Clarke's Sampler: A Technical and Historical Examination," in the files of the Valentine Museum.

Silk on linen ground; 20 1/2 in. x 18 1/8 in. Stitches: cross, outline, queen's.
Valentine Museum, V.84.122a

national enthusiasm generated by the visit of the Marquis de Lafayette in 1824 and 1825 (fig. 14). Lafayette was second only to George Washington as a popular Revolutionary war hero and symbol of American independence. Traveling throughout the country as a much older man, he arrived in Richmond, Virginia, for a week's sojourn on October 26, 1824. Mottoes and pictures commemorating Lafayette's return to America appeared in almost every imaginable medium. More typical than Anne's sampler were items such as ribbons, badges, and gloves, which were worn for the celebrations. Homes were opened and business operations suspended. Festivities included parades, races, banquets, and presentations. This sampler raises questions yet to be answered. Was Anne one of the school children presented to Lafayette upon his visit to Richmond? Where did she attend school?[14] How many other samplers were made to commemorate the event?

Figure 15. Sampler by William Levington, dated July 4, 1832; "Baltimore." Samplers worked by adult males are so rare that their numbers are not documented. Almost as rare are samplers worked by African-Americans of either gender.

Silk and crinkled silk on linen ground of 28 x 28 threads per in.; 22 1/8 in. x 21 1/4 in. Stitches: cross, satin.
1996-815

"Respectfully Presented"

During the nineteenth century the stitching and giving of samplers were appropriate methods of expressing one's emotions, whether the sentiment was gratitude, sorrow, protest, respect, affection, or friendship. Samplers, then, had become more than just schoolgirl stitching exercises: they served as metaphors.

William Levington worked an extraordinary sampler dated July 4, 1832 (figs. 15 and 16). Levington was an African-American pastor and founder of St. James First African Protestant Episcopal Church in Baltimore. Inscribed "Respectfully presented to James Bosley, Esq.," the embroidery honored James Bosley, a lawyer who, in 1825, had donated the land for the church building. The Reverend Mr. Levington served as rector of St. James, the first black Episcopal church south of the Mason-Dixon Line, from 1824 until his death in 1836. During his tenure, he directed day and Sunday schools for the neighborhood children.[15]

The patterns and motifs—a basket filled with flowers, floral border, and inscription—on Levington's sampler indicate that the embroidery is

Figure 16. Reverse side of figure 15. The difference between the colors on the obverse and reverse sides of this sampler shows the effects of the fugitive red dye, easily seen when the blue and white flowers on the front side, in figure 15, are contrasted with their purple and pink counterparts in this photograph.

clearly rooted in the American sampler-making tradition. Originally from New York, William Levington was ordained in Philadelphia in 1824 before he was sent to Baltimore to do missionary work. Interestingly, his embroidery bears a striking resemblance to a group of samplers worked in Philadelphia by schoolgirls (fig. 17). Known today as "Philadelphia presentation samplers," they represent a style that was popular until at least 1839.[16] Yet, Levington's sampler is set apart from typical schoolgirl needlework by its large-scale flowers, bold border, patterning on the basket, and ornamental peacock-head basket handles. This sampler, then, appears to be a synthesis of two different cultures and aesthetics.

The Reverend Mr. Levington could have expressed his gratitude in a number of conventional ways: he could have commissioned a piece of silver or furniture in Bosley's honor, written a poem, or presented a plaque. However, William Levington chose to demonstrate his appreciation through the intimate stitches of a sampler.

Figure 17 (opposite). Sampler by Ann Margaret Weaver, age twelve, dated December 24, 1816; "Philadelphia." Ann's is the earliest recorded example of the Philadelphia presentation samplers. She stitched: "Respectfully presented to Michael and Margaret Weaver by their affectionate daughter Ann Margaret Weaver."

Silk and crinkled silk on linen ground; 16 7/8 in. x 17 in. Stitches: bullion, chain, cross, outline, queen's, satin, stem. *Valentine Museum, V.75.299.9*

Joy and Sorrow
Still where rosy pleasure leads,
See a kindred grief pursue,
Behind the steps that misery treads,
Approaching comforts view.
The hues of bliss more brightly glow,
Chastis'd by sable tints of wo;
And blended form with artful strife,
The strength and harmony of life.
Philadelphia December 24th
Respectfully presented to Michael and Margaret Weaver by their affectionate
daughter Ann Margaret Weaver in the 13th year of her age 1816

Figure 18. Needlework picture, maker unknown, ca. 1660; England. This needlework picture is really a collection of isolated motifs, variations of which can be found in pattern books of the period.

Silk on silk satin with applied slips worked on linen; 16 in. x 11 3/8 in. Stitches: chain, couching, French knots, queen's, satin, straight, tent.

G1971-1483; Anonymous gift

TWO

"My Father Deare Paid for This That I Did Hear"

Any discussion of samplers, regardless of age and provenance, requires a review of their changing history and function to provide a framework for understanding the subject. What follows is a brief general review of the scholarship on sampler making in Britain, with relevant comments on European examples, as a context for understanding Virginia samplers.

The British sampler tradition—a tradition that had ties to Germany and the Netherlands—is an old one, with design and pattern antecedents found in Islamic Egyptian embroideries produced between the thirteenth and fifteenth centuries AD.[1] In Europe, pictorial and written evidence indicates that samplers or similar embroideries were stitched at least by the fifteenth century.[2] The nature of these very early samplers is confusing to say the least. While there is evidence to suggest that some were schoolgirl exercises, most seem to have been intended as records of patterns for specific embroidery on clothing and furnishings.[3] These pieces were worked by both adult women and professional male embroiderers. For example, Janet Arnold tells us that sample patterns of embroidery were prepared for Queen Elizabeth to choose from, as the following 1571 entry demonstrates: "Deleveryid to David Smyth our Enbrauderer One yerde of blak vellat [velvet] and half a yerde of blak Satten to make samplers. . . ."[4]

The Seventeenth Century

By the seventeenth century, samplers, typically long and narrow, were worked in two formats, known today as "spot" and "band." Consisting of scattered, isolated motifs of birds, animals, flowers, and geometric patterns, spot samplers may have derived from the practice of recording embroidery patterns for clothing, furnishings, and heraldic emblems (fig. 18).[5] Some of these samplers were probably experimental in nature; as a new stitch or pattern was learned it was added on to the sampler, which might have been rolled and tucked in a basket for easy storage. It could be unrolled later and used as a reference when doing mending, sewing, or more decorative needlework. What is not clear is the age of the makers of these spot samplers.

For purposes of the discussion of schoolgirl embroideries, it is the band sampler that most interests us. Band samplers are so named because of their characteristic horizontal bands of geometric patterns, flowers, vines, alphabets, and verses, nearly all of them worked in reversible stitches (fig. 20). Early in the seventeenth century band samplers were firmly established as part of a schoolgirl's curriculum (fig. 19).[6] Most of these embroideries were

Figure 19. Engraving from *Elementarwerke für die Jugend und ihre Freunde* [*Fundamentals for Young People and Their Friends*], authored by Bernhard Basedow, with engravings by Daniel Chodowiecki; Germany, 1774. Though printed a century later this engraving gives some idea of the setting in which sampler making—as well as other schoolgirl activities—was learned.
1962-221,53 (Tab. LII)

Figure 20A. Detail of Ann Taylor's sampler.

Figure 21. Detail of a sampler by Mary Swift, age nine, dated 1666; England. This wide pattern, consisting of stylized carnations, owls, and isolated figures of birds, dogs, and insects, is almost identical to the band illustrated in figure 20A, suggesting that Ann and Mary may have worked their pieces under the same school teacher.

Silk on linen of 53 x 48 threads per in.; 6 7/8 in. x 36 1/2 in. Stitches: bullion, couching, detached buttonhole, double running, eyelet, interlacing, long arm cross, marking cross, Montenegrin, outline, pattern darning, satin.
Private collection

Figure 20. Sampler by Ann Taylor, ca. 1666; England. Ann's band sampler is in the typical long and narrow format of English samplers of the seventeenth century. The inscriptions read: "Ann Taylor her work made in the year" and "She being born the 8 of Febry AD 1657."

Silk on linen of 54 x 46 threads per in.; 6 1/4 in. x 32 in. Stitches: bullion, couching, detached buttonhole, double running, eyelet, interlacing, long arm cross, marking cross, Montenegrin, outline, pattern darning, satin.
G1971-1483; Anonymous gift

worked under the direction of a teacher who designed them as well as provided the necessary instruction in needlework stitches. A needlework teacher often reused the same alphabets, patterns, and motifs throughout her teaching career, thus creating a clearly recognizable style unique to that individual teacher. Mary Swift's sampler, dated 1666, and Ann Taylor's, circa 1666, share identical alphabets and certain patterns arranged in such a way as to suggest that they were worked under the same teacher and probably finished in the same year (figs. 20A and 21).[7] The inscription on Mary Best's sampler, "John Best My Father Deare Paid for This That I Did Hear," reminds us that this education was limited to only those who could afford it (fig. 22).[8] In seventeenth-century England that economic group comprised, in addition to the aristocracy, the daughters of landed gentry, merchants, ministers, and successful tradesmen.

There are two distinct types of band samplers. Those worked in polychrome silk threads on a linen ground seem to have been the first of what was sometimes a series of needlework projects to be completed by a girl. The second type was stitched in techniques collectively labeled whitework, a term used in seventeenth-century records (fig. 23). Wrought on a white linen ground in white threads,

Figure 22. Sampler by Mary Best, dated September 16, 1693; England.

Silk on linen ground of 52 x 54 threads per in.; original dimensions 8 1/2 in. x 34 in. Stitches: bullion knots, buttonhole, chain, cross, detached buttonhole, double running, eyelet, French knots, four-sided, long arm cross, marking cross, running, satin, padded details.
1955-45 and 1955-46

Figure 22A. Detail of Mary Best's sampler. The wonderful three-dimensional figures of Adam and Eve are padded out with wool and wood.
1955-46

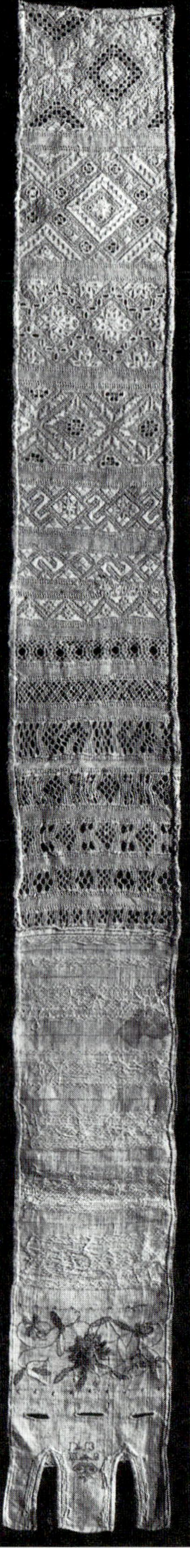

Figure 23. Sampler with initials MB, dated 1713; England. This whitework sampler was certainly not a beginner's piece and may well have been the second sampler in a series of needlework projects that MB worked.

Silk and linen on linen of 62 x 86 threads per in.; 3 5/8 in. x 32 in. Stitches: bullion, buttonhole, chain, detached buttonhole, double back stitch, filling, four-sided, hemstitch, herringbone, marking cross, outline, pattern darning, satin, woven and wrapped bars.
G1971-1657; Anonymous gift

usually linen and some silk, these embroideries feature cut and drawn work patterns in a variety of intricate stitches which produced beautiful lace-like results. Individual bands of whitework patterns also appear on polychrome samplers of this period.[9] The whitework sampler of nine-year-old Martha Edlin, dated 1669, was the second of three needlework projects which she worked between the years 1668 and 1671, her first being a polychrome band sampler dated 1668 and her final project a cabinet in raised work (fig. 24).[10] In this latter form, known today as stump work, areas were given three-dimensional qualities with stuffing, applied details, and/or areas of detached needle lace. Although these techniques are seen most often in seventeenth-century cabinets, caskets, and needlework pictures, Mary Best's sampler includes fine examples of this kind of work (fig. 22A).

What was the intent of these samplers? They were clearly learning exercises in stitches and

Figure 24. Box or toilet case with embroidered panels worked possibly by a member of the Whitton family, ca. 1665; possibly Tedington, England. This magnificent needlework box may have been the last of several needlework projects a school girl would have created. Wood and tortoise shell box measures 15 1/2 in. x 9 1/4 in. Embroidery on white silk satin weave ground with metallic purl, linen and silk threads, white metal, brass, pearls, and isinglass.

Stitches of the applied figures: buttonhole, bullion, coral knots, couching, detached buttonhole, encroaching satin, French knots, tent.
1956-300,A

needlework patterns, some of which would be needed by an adult female for taking care of the family textiles. Certainly the samplers reinforced the learning of alphabets and numbers, but whether a row of embroidered letters indicated that the stitcher was fully literate is another question. I would suggest, however, that these seventeenth-century samplers were rites of passage within a defined female sphere. They were worked by girls usually between the ages of nine and thirteen, by which time a girl probably would have reached puberty. With the completion of her first sampler, a young girl was recognized as ready to enter the domain of womanhood. She was ready to attempt more elaborate needlework projects and to begin learning the housewifery skills necessary for running a household. Her final needlework project not only represented her embroidery accomplishments but also signaled her entry into the adult female world.

The beauty of seventeenth-century samplers suggests to the modern observer that the original owners displayed them as demonstrations of young girls' proficiency in the needle arts. Yet unlike the beaded and raised work pictures, which were exhibited, we have no evidence that these samplers were ever framed during this time period. Interestingly, Mary Best's silk and raised work sampler of 1693, referred to above, was framed sometime in the eighteenth century. At that time, the thirty-four-inch sampler was cut in half to fit into separate frames.

The Eighteenth Century

On the other hand, period graphics, written documentation, and framing evidence all indicate that the practice of displaying samplers was well established early in the eighteenth century. The sampler evolved from a long, narrow piece—probably not intended to be framed—to a shorter, square or rectangular non-reversible sampler with decorative borders that could be framed and exhibited as the showpiece of a daughter's needlework accomplishments.[11] British samplers of this era usually feature precise embroidery and symmetrical motifs. Worsted grounds are common, as are the inclusion of crowns or coronets and isolated motifs. Mary Victor's sampler of 1764 certainly falls into the category of neat and precise, although not exactly symmetrical, embroidery (fig. 25). Some of the isolated motifs, such as the milking maid, are also seen in Dutch samplers of the same period.[12] She unintentionally accommodated the modern viewer by identifying the coronets with initials for baronet, viscount, earl, and duke. Also notable is the wonderful detailing of a door handle in detached buttonhole stitch on the centered Georgian-style house.

Figure 25. Sampler by Mary Victor, dated 1764; England. Precise embroidery on a fine wool ground is typical of English samplers.
Silk on worsted ground of 51 x 45 threads per in.; 12 1/8 in. x 12 7/8 in. Stitches: cross, detached buttonhole, eyelet, hem, outline.
1989-332

Forty years later, in 1803, Elizabeth Weston depicted the unusual figure of a harlequin on her sampler (figs. 26 and 26A). Harlequin, a comic character that originated in the Italian Commedia dell'Arte, is more typically seen, along with other Commedia dell'Arte characters, in Meissen and Chelsea porcelain figures of the 1740s. Pantomimes in the harlequinade tradition continued to be written as late as the 1790s in England, with performances at Covent Garden, Drury Lane, and other small theaters.[13] These plays may well have been the inspiration for the figure on this sampler as well as other textiles of the period.[14]

Scottish samplers of the late eighteenth and early nineteenth centuries are noted for their inclusion of family initials, especially those of the mother's maiden name (fig. 27). Hearts, peacocks, and a border of twisted stems can also point to a Scottish origin. A third clue to a possible Scottish provenance lies in the materials, specifically the use of red and green crewel or silk embroidery thread on a worsted or linen ground (fig. 28).

It is important to note that some Virginia samplers contain family initials and Scottish surnames, an inclusion that makes misidentification easy, especially if no place of origin is inscribed on the sam-

Figure 26A. Detail of Elizabeth Weston's sampler. The unusual harlequin figure in the bottom right corner may have been inspired by a theatrical character.

Figure 26. Sampler by Elizabeth Weston, dated March 7, 1803; England.
Silk on worsted ground of 54 x 54 threads per in.; 12 3/8 in. x 17 1/4 in. Stitches: cross, satin.
1995-208; Purchased with partial funds from the Antique Collectors' Guild and the Williamsburg Rose and Thistle Chapter of the Embroiderers' Guild of America

pler. Two samplers, now thought to be Scottish, were originally identified as Virginia work because of genealogical research that located one of the girls with the same name in a prominent family of Norfolk, Virginia (figs. 29 and 30).[15] Jannet Nimmo and Catherine Bett worked their samplers in 1812 and 1825, respectively, on tammy grounds. Of particular interest is the use of chenille threads on the tree trunks, which gives them a soft, velvety pile (fig. 30A). Jannet also used a bead for the peacock's eye. These samplers, with their similar materials, compositions, frames, stretchers, and melancholy verses flanked by neo-classical swags, were certainly worked under the tutelage of the same unidentified

Figure 27. Sampler by Ann Hill, ca. 1800; possibly Scotland. Ann included what are probably her parents' initials, WH and EH, at the right bottom corner of her sampler. With the purchase of this piece in 1930, Colonial Williamsburg began its sampler collection.
Silk and wool on worsted ground of 52 x 52 threads per in.;
8 in. x 12 in. Stitches: cross.
1930-377

Figure 28. Sampler by Catherine Blair, dated 1831; attributed to Scotland. The crowns with initials AB and MB are probably for Catherine's parents. Four and one-half lines of other initials, probably for family and friends, appear in the center of the embroidery.
Silk and wool on linen ground of 32 x 31 threads per in.;
12 1/2 in. x 17 1/8 in. Stitches: chain, cross, double running, eyelet.
1983-226

Figure 29. Sampler by Jannet Nimmo, dated 1812; possibly Scotland.

Silk and silk chenille on worsted ground of 46 by 45 threads per in.; 21 5/8 in. x 14 3/8 in. Stitches: back, buttonhole, chain, couched, cross, double cross, outline, satin, surface satin, tent.
1989-365

Figure 30. Sampler by Catherine Bett, dated 1825; possibly Scotland. Figure 29 and this piece were certainly worked under the instruction of the same unknown teacher.

Silk and silk chenille on worsted ground of 58 by 55 threads per in.; 23 3/8 in. x 14 5/8 in. Stitches: back, buttonhole, chain, couched, cross, flat, herringbone, outline, satin, tent.
G1990-21; Purchased with funds given by Mr. And Mrs. Howard Via

Figure 30A. Detail of Catherine Bett's sampler. The chenille threads in the tree trunks give them a soft, velvety pile.

instructor. A Scottish emigrant needlework teacher working in Virginia has not been entirely ruled out. However, it seems more likely that these samplers have a Scottish origin because recently they have been associated with another documented Scottish sampler worked by Elizabeth Muirhead in 1828.[16]

Among the most practical forms of embroidery found in European work are darning samplers and workbooks. Darning samplers represent a form that is rarely seen in American needlework (fig. 31).[17] Their origins can be found in German, Dutch, and Danish work of the mid-eighteenth century. These were practice pieces intended to teach mending techniques. Instead of the usual alphabets, numbers,

Figure 31. Sampler by M. Wigg, ca. 1775–1800; Great Britain. A darning sampler such as this example was an exercise in darning patterns. Knowing how to darn was useful in the repair of woven household textiles.

Silk on linen ground of 68 x 62 threads per in.; 14 1/4 in. square. Stitches: chain, cross, hem, outline, pattern darning.
G1971-1488; Anonymous gift

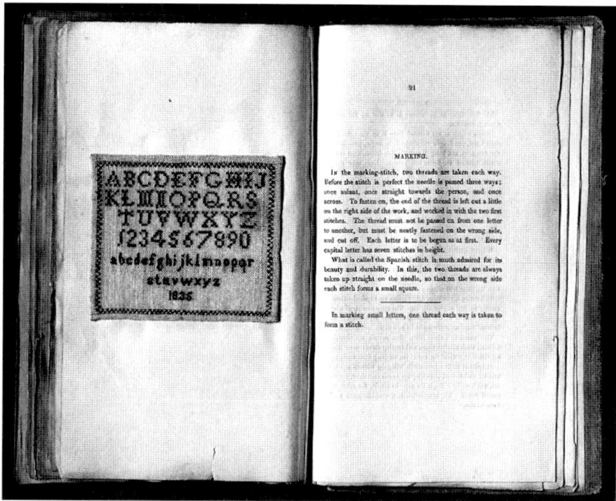

21

MARKING.

In the marking-stitch, two threads are taken each way. Before the stitch is perfect the needle is passed three ways; once aslant, once straight towards the person, and once across. To fasten on, the end of the thread is left out a little on the right side of the work, and worked in with the two first stitches. The thread must not be passed on from one letter to another, but must be neatly fastened on the wrong side, and cut off. Each letter is to be begun as at first. Every capital letter has seven stitches in height.

What is called the Spanish stitch is much admired for its beauty and durability. In this, the two threads are always taken up straight on the needle, so that on the wrong side each stitch forms a small square.

In marking small letters, one thread each way is taken to form a stitch.

Figure 32. *Instructions on Needlework and Knitting*; printed in London, 1832. Written on cover: "N.S. Central Sch." This manual consists of useful sewing lessons such as hemming, filling, darning, and gathering. The book is opened to a lesson on marking linens and shows a completed marking sampler, which measures only 3 5/8 in. x 3 in. Interestingly, the instructions given for Spanish stitch are not for the double running stitch of the seventeenth century but rather for a reversible four-sided stitch.
G1971-1633; Anonymous gift

and verses, the stitcher simulated different fabric weaves in embroidery. In the more complex darning samplers, small areas were actually cut out of the sampler cloth and the hole filled in with two or more colors darned into a pattern. These exercises came in handy in repairing the family's woven textiles. An instruction book of 1832 tells us: "The needles used for darning are made very long and thin" and "[h]ard twisted cotton or silk will not do well for darning."[18]

By the first half of the nineteenth century needlework exercise books were common in many British schools. These books consisted of practical needlework lessons such as marking, hemming, shirtmaking, darning, and knitting. Opposite each of the lessons was a place for the student's completed work to be stitched, pinned, or glued (fig. 32). Some needlework books with completed projects were actually manuals used by teachers "for promoting the education of the poor in the principles of the established church."[19] In addition to needlework lessons, one English workbook of 1832 gave the following instructions for the teachers: "As the beauty of needle-work consists in its regularity and cleanliness, every child must be taught to wash her hands before she begins. . . ."[20] In Britain, by the second half of the nineteenth century, most sampler making was done in orphanages or schools for the poor (fig. 33). As the curricula for a female education became more academic, the popularity of the sampler declined.

Figure 33. Frontispiece from *The Workwoman's Guide*; published in England, 1838. "She stretcheth out her hand to the Poor. — / She looketh well to the ways of her Household. Provs 31 Ch." By the second half of the nineteenth century most sampler making was done in orphanages or schools for the poor.
John D. Rockefeller, Jr. Library (TT 705.L27 1838), Colonial Williamsburg Foundation

Designs

Designs for British and European samplers were available from a number of sources.[21] From the fifteenth through the seventeenth centuries, textiles and carpets imported from the Orient as well as

Figure 34. Box, seventeenth century; Italy or France. The stylized flowers and vase seen on the lid of this small box are similar to those found on samplers of the period.
Paper form with woven silk and applied straw lining.
3 in. diameter; 3/4 in. high.
G1971-1702,1; Anonymous gift

those of European manufacture inspired motifs (fig. 34).[22] Pattern books, published as early as 1523, provided suitable design sources for a variety of needlework techniques, from lace to whitework to needlework pictures and samplers. These books were reissued throughout the sixteenth, seventeenth, and eighteenth centuries with favorite patterns borrowed back and forth. One of the most popular pattern books of the 1600s was engraver Johan Sibmacher's *Schon Neues Modelbuch*, first published in Nurnberg in 1597. After Sibmacher's death in 1611, his wife and heirs reprinted the designs and then sold them to another printer, Paulus Fürst, in 1653. These patterns continued to show up in works from various German publishing houses throughout the seventeenth and eighteenth centuries, until 1806.[23] Several motifs from Sibmacher's book, including a majestic peacock, are reproduced on a German sampler of 1734 that, incidentally, measures the astounding length of 84 1/2 inches (figs. 35, 35A–B, 36A–C). It is worked in a format of patterned bands and single motifs that include figures of men, women, animals, and flowers. Although designs similar to printed patterns can be found on English samplers of the seventeenth century, it is not until the eighteenth that English samplers display exact copies of those patterns.[24]

Some of the motifs on English spot samplers may have been drawn by the embroiderer or professional artists may have been hired.[25] To transfer designs from pattern books and other sources onto the sampler cloth, holes were pricked in the outline of the paper design. A powder was then dusted across the pricked design and pounced, or pushed, through the holes to the underlying cloth. The outline was then completed by connecting the dots with ink using a small brush. Though published in the next century, Hannah Robertson's 1777 description of a similar process in *The Young Ladies School of Arts* bears repeating:

> Ladies who have not a genius for drawing or painting, may procure good patterns, and clap them on a pane of glass in the window, placing a sheet of fine paper above it, and with a black lead pencil trace all the outlines which done prick it with a fine needle, then place it on the silk or cloth you intend to draw; powder a little coal, or wood burnt to coal, very fine, put it in a piece of thin cloth, and pounce it thro' the holes of your pattern, and you will have the figure compleat; draw it with gunpowder beat fine and mixed with milk; as blue, &c. is difficult to wash out.[26]

One rare surviving pattern book is a leather-bound volume consisting of 113 engraved sheets of animals, birds, fish, flowers, fruits, nuts, and composite designs by various hands including John Dunstall, Robert Gaywood, John Chantrey, and William Vaughan. A portion of the manual consists of *A Booke of all Kinds of Beasts. . .*, printed and sold by Robert Walton at the Globe & Compasses, St. Paul's Churchyard, circa 1675–1685. Some of the sheets have been repaired, some removed, and a few figures have been cut out. One page clearly shows signs of pricking (fig. 37). That said, the overall condition is better than might be expected of an evidently well used pattern book of the period.

Materials

The common ground fabric for seventeenth-century English samplers was a plain weave linen. A plain worsted weave, known as tammy, was a popular ground for British samplers in the 1700s. Eighteenth-century Dutch sampler makers used cotton or grounds with linen warps and cotton wefts. Most samplers from about 1600 to 1850 were worked in silk embroidery threads. Metallic threads were incorporated in a few rare and obviously more expensive samplers, and linen threads were used in

Figure 35. Sampler, initials MSB, dated 1734; Germany. This sampler is worked completely in reversible stitches, creating a backside that is a mirror image of the front.

Silk on pieced linen ground of 33 x 33 threads per in.; 12 3/8 in. x 84 1/2 in. Stitches: cross, double running, four-sided.
G1971-1480; Anonymous gift

Figure 35A. Detail of German sampler. The top band features a pair of mermen and a cartouche containing the worker's initials and the year of completion. The bottom band shows a reclining stag flanked by vases of flowers. Though not illustrated here, these vase arrangements are also from Sibmacher's *Schon Neues Modelbuch*.

Figure 35B. Detail of German sampler. A mirror image of this peacock is found in the first edition of Sibmacher's pattern book.

Figures 36A, B, C. From top to bottom, merman with half-cartouche, reclining stag, and peacock, all from Sibmacher's *Schon Neues Modelbuch*, 1597.

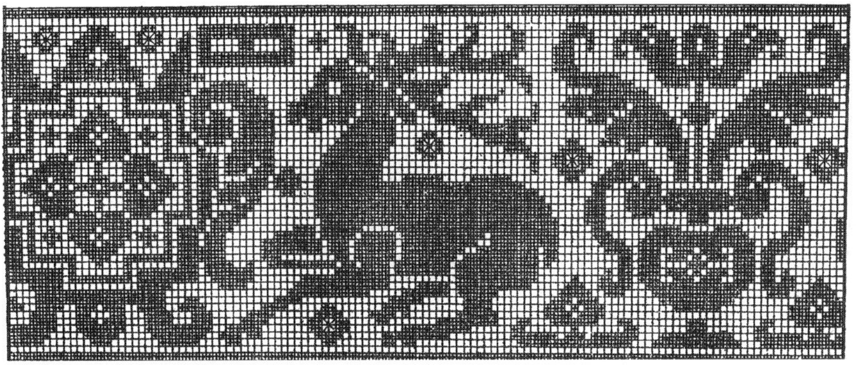

whitework examples of the 1600s. A few exceptional samplers of this century included beads or raised work areas stuffed with bits of wool, cotton, or wood (fig. 22A). Some samplers of the later eighteenth and early nineteenth century feature chenille threads, sequins, and painted areas.[27] Wool embroidery threads were used in the 1700s, but cotton thread and cotton grounds were not common until the nineteenth century.

Figure 37. Page from a pattern book printed and sold by Robert Walton, ca. 1675–1685; London. The pricked outline of the flower has been modified, with the stem lengthened and some leaves omitted.
John D. Rockefeller, Jr. Library (MS96.17), Colonial Williamsburg Foundation

Stitches

Many different stitches and techniques—too numerous to describe adequately here—were worked on samplers. English samplers of the 1600s consist of a larger variety of complicated stitches than those of succeeding centuries. In particular reversible stitches such as the four-sided, eyelet, double running, and marking cross were predominant on English band samplers of this period, as well as on some eighteenth-century German samplers (fig. 35).[28]

Of particular relevance to our discussions of Virginia samplers is the marking stitch. The marking cross stitch, or reversible cross stitch, is created with six passes of the needle, beginning with a diagonal stitch. In order to make the cross reversible, a straight stitch must next be worked before the final diagonal stitch. The cross can be started from any of the four corner holes (fig. 38).[29]

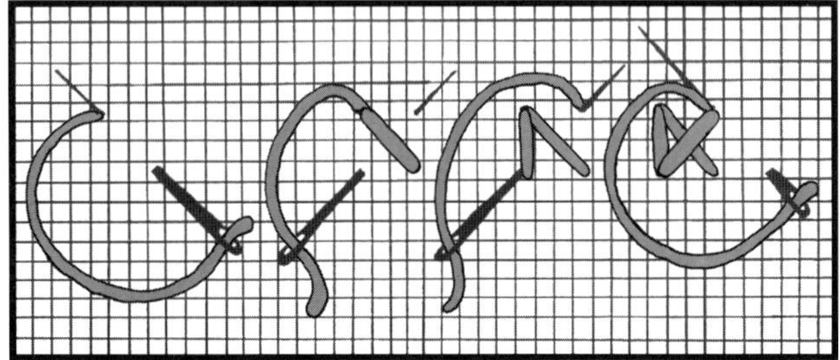

Figure 38. Marking stitch

What was the need for these reversible stitches? Valuable household linens including tablecloths and napkins, and even clothing such as shifts and shirts, were embroidered with numbers and initials in order to keeps sets together and to ensure that items sent out to be laundered or mended were returned to their proper owner (fig. 39). In the eighteenth century this was still a concern, as Susanna Whatman indicated in her housekeeping book of 1776: "All linen should be marked according to its purpose, its number and the year besides the name. This saves a great deal of trouble with house linen."[30] A mark that could be read from both sides was obviously more attractive than one that could not. Seen on early British, German, and colonial American samplers, the marking stitch was all but obsolete by the mid-eighteenth century—except in Virginia, where it appears on samplers from several different regional groups and as late as the 1810s.[31] ❦

Figure 39. Inventory pillow by Jane Jamson, dated October 18, 1824; Aberdeen, Scotland. This inventory pillow was used to track various household and personal textiles probably as they were sent back and forth to the laundry. A straight pin was used to mark the appropriate number of pieces.

Silk on a worsted ground of 44 x 44 threads per in.; 6 1/4 in. x 7 1/2 in. Stitches: cross.
1985-228

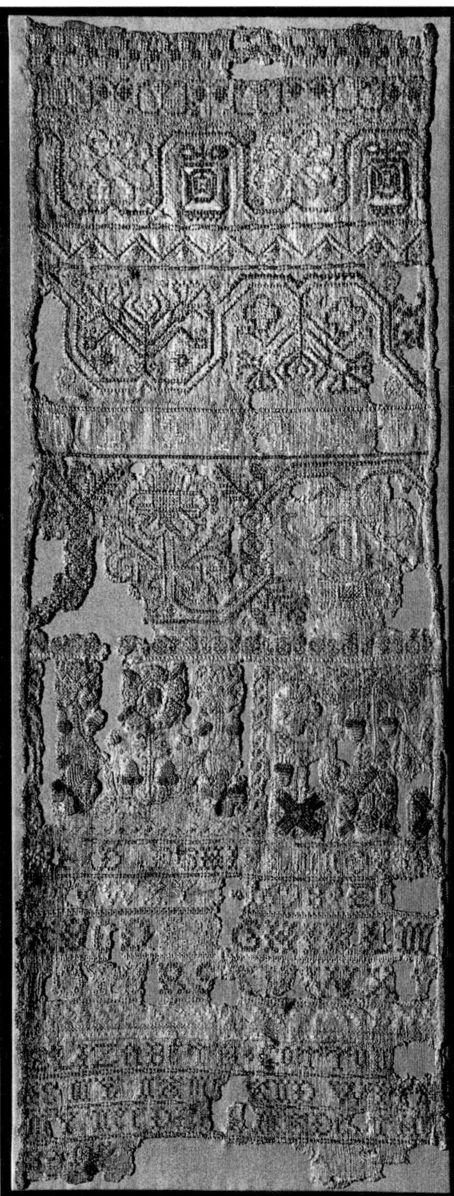

Figure 40. Sampler by Elizabeth Cotton, dated 1698; attributed to Portsmouth, Massachusetts Bay Colony. Elizabeth is probably the Elizabeth Cotton who was the third child of William Cotton, a farmer, innholder, and gentleman of Portsmouth. She married William Fernald on July 31, 1707 (Noyes, Libby, and Davis, *Genealogical Dictionary of Maine and New Hampshire*, p. 164). I am indebted to Kathleen Epstein for this research.

Silk and linen on linen ground of 41 x 43 threads per in.; 9 1/4 in. x 24 1/8 in. Stitches: cross, double running, eyelet, four-sided, hem, knotted detached buttonhole, marking cross, reversible long arm cross, satin, stem.
G1994-81; Partial gift of Betty Skarohlid

Figure 41. Sampler by Ann Almy, age ten, dated 1733; attributed to Newport, Rhode Island. First published in Bolton and Coe, *American Samplers*, pl. 112, it was mistakenly recorded as dated 1783. This incorrect late date puzzled scholars for years (see Ring, *Let Virtue Be a Guide to Thee*, pp. 64–67).

Silk on linen ground of 30 x 34 threads per in.; 8 in. x 19 in. Stitches: back, cross, eyelet, four-sided, herringbone, marking cross, queen's, tent.
1992-11

THREE

"There is a Boarding School opened in this town"

NEEDLEWORK SKILLS AND the sampler-making tradition made their transference to America with the early colonists. By 1650 girls in the Plymouth and Massachusetts Bay Colonies were working samplers.[1] These early American examples resembled English band samplers in their general size, shape, and format (fig. 40). Some were patterned with letters, numbers, and decorative designs worked in polychrome silk threads. Others were worked in white threads on white grounds using cut and drawn work patterns. Just like their English cousins, most were embroidered in reversible stitches—each stitch counted over three threads of the fabric—so that the outlines of the patterns were seen on both the fronts and backs of the embroideries.

EARLY CHANGES IN AMERICAN SAMPLERS

From the end of the seventeenth century through the first forty years of the eighteenth, four major developments occurred in American sampler making. First, the activity spread from New England to as far south as Charleston, South Carolina.[2] Second, the technique of stitching over three threads shifted to a count of two threads, the latter still common today. Third, by the 1730s American samplers throughout the colonies began to take on their own distinct identity. In addition to the change in technique, they became typically less formal and symmetrical than contemporary English samplers. During the 1700s the sampler shape also evolved from a long, narrow piece—usually not intended to be framed—to a shorter, more rectangular, but sometimes square, sampler that could be framed and displayed as the showpiece of a girl's needlework accomplishments.

The fourth and most significant change during these decades was in the reversibility of patterns. While reversible stitches were still worked in isolated bands, entire samplers were no longer made in reversible patterns.[3] Instead, design efforts were concentrated on the front of the work. This change resulted in a decrease in labor investment, which became even more evident as the century progressed. This transition, however, did not take place in most eighteenth-century Virginia samplers: these embroideries exhibit reversible stitches and neat, mirror-image backs.[4]

Not only did a distinct American form of sampler appear but, as a whole, regional styles and characteristics developed in American needlework, just as they did in American furniture. An illustrative example is Ann Almy's sampler of 1733, which belongs to the earliest group of samplers from Newport, Rhode Island (fig. 41). The bold central floral motif in the second decorative band of Ann's work is found on other Newport samplers made between 1725 and 1749. The repetition of this pattern suggests that the samplers were made under the same anonymous Newport teacher.[5] However, at this early date, Ann's sampler clings to the English band format and precise needlework.

THE ACCOMPLISHED MISS

Throughout the eighteenth century young girls whose families could afford it usually received some type of formal education (fig. 42). This instruction was ultimately aimed at preparing girls for marriage and the roles of wife, mistress of a house, and mother. Children as young as three attended grammar or dame schools where classes were taught by women in their homes. Here, in addition to elementary

Figure 42. *The Schoolmistress / La Maitresse D'Ecole*, hand-colored mezzotint, dated 1804; London. The English version of the poem reads as follows: "In every village mark'd with little spire. / Embowr'd in trees and hardly know to fame. / There dwells, in lowly shades and mean attire. / A matron old, whom we schoolmistress name. / Who boasts unruly brats with birch to tame."
1975-126

Figure 43. Sampler by Sarah Araline Huse, age six, dated 1813; America. This embroidery may have been the first of a series of needlework projects she worked.
Silk on linen ground of 33 x 29 threads per in.; 6 3/8 in. x 9 3/8 in. Stitches: cross, eyelet variation, hem.
G1974-685; Bequest of Grace Hartshorn Westerfield

reading, simple arithmetic, and knitting, they learned plain sewing by working a modest sampler (fig. 43).[6]

Especially by the last decades of the eighteenth century, more fortunate girls went on to encounter specialized teachers and advanced needlework instruction at schools not always in their hometowns (fig. 45). They could have boarded at the school or with friends or family. Such institutions may have boasted a curriculum similar to that offered at Mrs. Brough's female seminary, which she proposed opening in Petersburg, Virginia, in 1805. She intended to include the following:

> universally esteemed branches proper to complete the education of young females, viz. open needle-work of every description, landscape painting, tambouring, sculpture, and even embroidery, together with equally useful branches of polite education, viz. English grammar, reading, writing, arithmetic, and geography. She hopes to meet the encouragement, and pledges herself that proper attention will be paid to the morals of those entrusted to her charge. . . .[7]

That needlework teachers paid strict attention to the morals of their students is evident not only from advertisements such as this one, but also from the pious verses found on so many samplers of the late eighteenth and early nineteenth centuries. These poems reflected an awareness of the proper behavior that society expected of its daughters.

Completed needlework projects were brought home and proudly displayed by parents as proof of the girl's needlework accomplishments as well as her diligence and virtue (fig. 44). The more elaborate samplers and embroideries also made a distinct social statement, proclaiming that the needleworker's family was at a social and financial level sufficient to afford to send her to school and pay for expensive embroidery materials.

The Teachers

Inventive needlework instructors, each teaching her own unique sampler patterns and techniques,

Figure 44. *Farmer Giles & his Wife showing off their daughter Betty to their Neighbours on her return from School*, engraving, dated January 1, 1809; published in London. Although this is a satire on the education of females during the first part of the nineteenth century, it does represent a scene that was common in both England and America. Parents welcomed their daughters home from boarding schools by showing off their accomplishments in hopes of enticing an appropriate suitor. Notice that in the print Betty's sampler of 1808 is proudly displayed on the wall of her parents' parlor.
Photograph courtesy British Museum

Figure 45. Needlework Picture, "Scipio Restoring The Captive Lady," by Harriet Cowles, age sixteen, dated 1806; possibly Connecticut. Harriet more than likely worked this magnificent silk embroidery, representing the culmination of years of needlework instruction, at a boarding school near her hometown of Farmington, Connecticut. Although the needlework has yet to be attributed to a specific teacher, similar frames have been found on pictures known to have been worked at Mrs. Lydia Royse's and the Misses Pattens' schools in Hartford, Connecticut (see Ring, *Girlhood Embroidery*, pp. 205–213, for similar frames). Harriet died of a "prevailing fever" two years after she completed this picture. It descended in the family and, in the second half of the nineteenth century, apparently was carried by her brother's family to Virginia, where it was found in 1992 (Calvin Duvall Cowles, comp., *Genealogy of the Cowles Families in America*, vol. 1, pp. 133, 288, 289, 564, 565).

Silk, chenille and metallic threads, brass spangles, and watercolor on silk in a gilt and gessoed white pine frame with black eglomisé (reverse painting on glass) mat. Framed size: 31 1/2 in. x 33 1/4 in. Stitches: couching, flat, French knots, herringbone, outline, satin, stem.
1992-101, A-B

established recognizable spheres of influence in sampler making throughout the colonies. Some of these teachers were young women who taught to support themselves until marriage. Others were widows, sometimes working with their daughters, trying to eke out a living. For many unmarried women, the role of schoolmistress was the only alternative to the reliance on charity from family, friends, the community, or the church. An 1834 editorial commented on this dilemma:

> WHAT can she do? There are but very few avenues of business in which women are privileged to walk. The wages for female labor is very trifling; and when she has others besides herself to provide for, it seems almost impossible that a woman can succeed.[8]

In hopes of attracting students, teachers advertised themselves as being "just from England" or as "teaching in the English style." For example, in 1772 Miss Wright informed the gentlemen and ladies of Fredericksburg, Virginia:

> there is a BOARDING SCHOOL opened in this town for Young Ladies by Miss Wright, from England, who undertakes to instruct the following branches, VIZ. READING, WRITING, ARITHMETIC, DRESDEN, TENTWORK, SHELLWORK, and all kinds of NEEDLEWORK. . . .[9]

Her terms for teaching also included boarding and washing—just two of the ways a teacher might supplement her income. Newspaper advertisements indicate that some teachers moved from one city to another looking for employment and more prosperous times. In 1795 Mrs. Bell from Charleston advertised in Alexandria that she taught "Reading and Writing, with correctness, Plain Work, Marking, Open Work and Embroidery."[10] In 1797 she had moved to Norfolk and in 1799 she was in Richmond, once again advertising as being from Charleston.[11]

The enduring styles of some sampler groups suggest, on the other hand, that certain teachers taught continuously for years in one region. Clearly the economic lot of many of these teachers was in sharp contrast to the affluence of their students.[12]

American Regionalism

During the eighteenth century, the trend of schoolgirl embroidery was away from the style of horizontal patterns arranged in a narrow vertical format and towards a much freer, more original sampler with considerable variety in design and technique (figs. 46 and 46A). This direction continued into the early 1800s, resulting in a smorgasbord of sampler styles: Massachusetts hunting and pastoral scenes (figs. 47, 48, 49); New York biblical samplers (fig. 50); Canterbury baskets (figs. 51 and 51A); Portsmouth houses and barns (figs. 53 and 53A); Pennsylvania-German stars (fig. 52); New Jersey wide-eyed stags (figs. 54 and 54A); and Maryland florals (figs. 55, 55A, 56, 56A). The assortment of sampler designs was as vast as the teacher's imagination and the student's skill.

Any attempt here to specify or describe all the identified groups of sampler styles is redundant; researchers such as Mary Jaene Edmonds, Glee Krueger, Betty Ring, and Susan Burrows Swan have successfully accomplished this on a much larger scale.[13] In addition to their encyclopedic works, numerous museum catalogs and magazine articles have characterized the needlework associated with a particular school or region. The illustrations presented earlier in this chapter—all from the textile collection at Colonial Williamsburg—are merely a few of the examples of the diversity of sampler groups that have been researched. These as well as the following three Chesapeake-area groups will provide the reader with models for understanding Virginia schoolgirl work.

Figure 46. Sampler by Sarah Salter, age twelve, dated 1779; attributed to Newburyport, Massachusetts. Sarah's whimsical cow munching on daisies clearly illustrates the originality and individualism seen in American needlework during this period. Hannah Johnson's 1768 sampler, inscribed "Newbury," may be the earliest of this group (Bolton and Coe, *American Samplers*, pl. 24). A later piece worked by Ann Poore, ca. 1782, depicts a similar cow and the same verse that appears on Sarah's sampler (*Important Americana*, lot 189).

Silk on linen ground of 30 x 32 threads per in.; 18 in. x 17 1/2 in. Stitches: cross, double running, eyelet, flat, outline, satin, tent.
1961-47

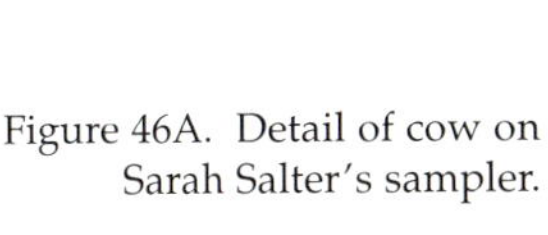

Figure 46A. Detail of cow on Sarah Salter's sampler.

Figure 47. Sampler by Mary Starker, age eleven, dated 1760; "Newbury," Massachusetts. Mary's sampler belongs to an early group of Newbury samplers characterized by large blue vases, sawtooth bands, bold stylized floral bands, and animals and fruit trees in the bottom section. This sampler, known as the "Chase Sampler" because of the running deer at the bottom, was offered by Colonial Williamsburg as an adapted needlework kit from 1967 to 1997. For similar works, see Ring, *Girlhood Embroidery*, vol. 1, pp. 114–116.

Silk on linen ground of 46 x 44 threads per in.; 15 1/2 in. x 23 in. Stitches: chain, cross, eyelet, French knots, queen's, outline, satin, tent.
1961-57

Figure 48. Sampler by Mary Welsh, age eleven, ca. 1770; attributed to Boston, Massachusetts. Mary was the daughter of John Welsh, a Boston jeweler, and Mary Parker. In 1774 her sister Grace worked a similar needlework sampler, location now unknown, which is illustrated in Bolton and Coe, *American Samplers*, pl. 25. These embroideries are characteristic of Boston samplers made between 1760 and 1790. They feature motifs such as the reclining shepherdess, pole-vaulter, spotted black dog, and trio of sheep—two white and one black (for examples similar to the style of Mary Welsh's embroidery, see Bolton and Coe, *American Samplers*, pls. 26, 38, and 106). Moreover, these motifs typically are found on the Boston "fishing lady" needlework pictures, a group so named by Helen Bowen because of the dominant figure of a lady fishing. This term has come to encompass a variety of pastoral scenes in canvas and crewelwork. For examples, see Helen Bowen, "The Fishing Lady and Boston Common," pp. 70–73; Nancy Graves Cabot, "The Fishing Lady and Boston Common," pp. 28–31, and "Engravings and Embroideries: The Sources of Some Designs in the Fishing Lady Pictures," pp. 367–369; Ring, *Girlhood Embroidery*, vol. 1, pp. 45–53.

Silk on linen ground of 32 x 26 threads per in.; 16 3/4 in. x 23 in. Stitches: detached buttonhole, eyelet, French knots, herringbone, marking cross, outline, satin.
1962-309

Figure 49. Needlework picture, attributed to Mary Woodhull, age nine, ca. 1755. Written in ink on the stretcher: "Worked by Mary Woodhull b. 10 July 1745 d. 19 Oct. 1815 daughter of Richard & Elizabeth (Smith) Woodhull. Mary married 20 Mar 1774 Amos Underhill of Flushing L.I. issue two children." If family history is correct in attributing this picture to Mary Woodhull of New York, then she probably worked it while attending a Boston boarding school, where pastoral scenes such as this were commonly taught. (See Cabot, "The Fishing Lady and Boston Common," p. 30, fig. 5, for an almost identical picture.)

Crewel on linen ground of 24 x 26 threads per in.; 25 3/4 in. x 21 1/4 in. Stitches: French knots, tent.
1961-50

Figure 50. Sampler by Mary Ogilvie, age nine, dated 1768; New York City. Born in 1759, Mary Margaret Ogilvie was the daughter of Catharine Susanna Symes and John Ogilvie. Her father became the assistant pastor of Trinity Church in 1764. Mary's sampler consists of five biblical vignettes possibly derived from Dutch delft tiles. The scenes have been identified by Betty Ring and Dorothy McCoach: (from top left to bottom right) Adam and Eve; fruit tree; the Sower or possibly Elijah feeding the ravens; Jesus resting before feeding the multitudes; and Jacob's ladder. Although these religious scenes are obscure to many today, in the eighteenth century biblical stories such as these were part of a religious vocabulary recognized by most schoolgirls. Mary's work belongs to a group of colonial New York City samplers dating between 1746 and 1768, most of which were worked by the daughters of Trinity Church parishioners. Besides the religious vignettes, the samplers are characterized by solidly worked grounds and deeply arcaded, tripartite borders. This style may have originated in New Rochelle, New York, at one of the French boarding schools for girls (Ring, *Girlhood Embroidery*, vol. 2, pp. 294, 296–303; and Ring, *Joan Stephens Collection*, lot 2060).

Silk and metallic on linen ground of 36 x 34 threads per in.; 16 1/2 in. x 15 3/8 in. Stitches: cross, queen's, satin.
G1979-57; Gift of Mrs. Edwin J. Phelps

Figure 51. Sampler by Martha B. Horn, age eleven, ca. 1824; probably Gilmanton, New Hampshire. Although Martha did not stitch the characteristic green leafy plume so common on samplers from the Canterbury region, her sampler does include certain features associated with this group: undulating hillocks, birds, centered woven basket with reverse-S side handles, and major motifs outlined in black silk thread. This large group of samplers, made between 1786 and 1833, has been instrumental in providing evidence that some women in Canterbury made a career of teaching. For further information, see essays by Elisabeth Donaghy Garrett and co-authors Theodore Mitchell and Heather Caldwell in *Lessons Stitched in Silk: Samplers from the Canterbury Region of New Hampshire*; and Ring, *Girlhood Embroidery*, vol. 1, pp. 230–235.

Silk on linen ground of 24 x 24 threads per in.; 21 1/2 in. x 16 1/2 in. Stitches: chain, cross, eyelet, outline, satin.
1994-45

Figure 51A. Detail of basket of flowers on Martha Horn's sampler

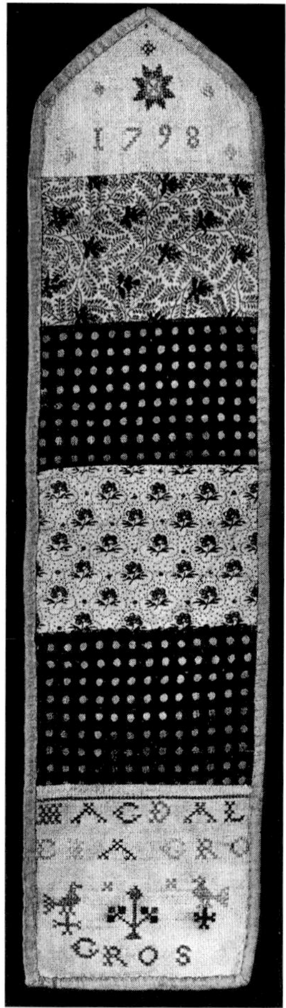

Figure 52. Sewing case by Magdalena Gros, dated 1798; probably Bucks County, Pennsylvania. This thread and needle case has five pockets for holding thread. It is embellished in cross stitch with small, angular motifs similar to those found on Pennsylvania German needlework. Magdalena was probably a Franconia Mennonite from the Deep Runn congregation (Tandy and Charles Hersh, *Samplers of the Pennsylvania Germans*, p. 215).

Silk on linen ground of 40 x 48 threads per in. with printed cottons and striped linen backing; 3 7/8 in. x 14 1/2 in. Stitches: cross.
G1958-181; Gift of Ernest LoNano

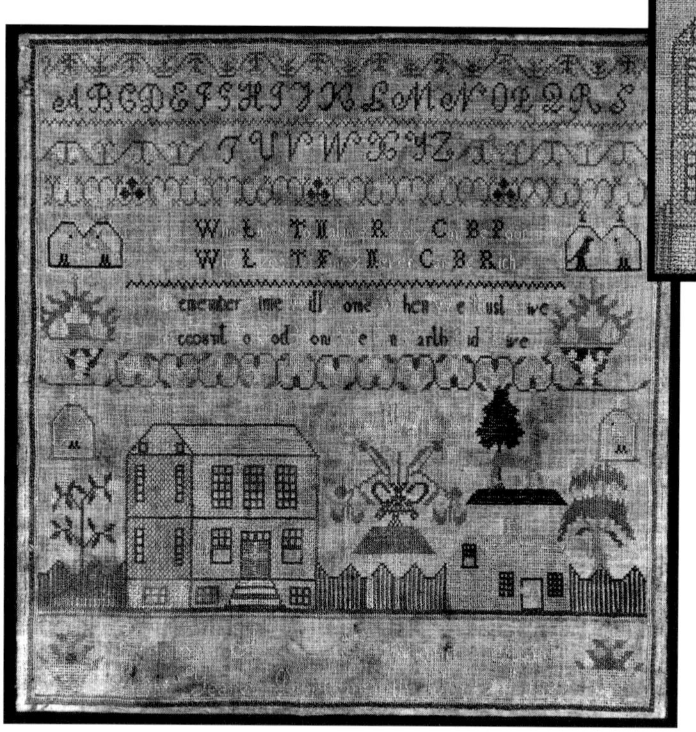

Figure 53A. Detail of two-storied house in Emeline Howland's sampler.

Figure 53. Sampler by Emeline A. Howland, age eight, dated October 27, 1827; "Portsmouth," New Hampshire. Emeline's work belongs to the largest recognizable group of Portsmouth samplers, all stitched between 1818 and 1840. They are characterized by a prominently placed two-storied house, fence, and barn. The open windows of the house are unusual for samplers from this group; however, they are a feature, as is the double birdcage, of Virginia samplers. Emeline was born in West Barnstable on February 27, 1819, to Jabez and Hannan Parker Howland. Her father filled various local offices and represented the town several years at the General Court. Emeline married Frederic Parker on September 2, 1838. They lived in Barnstable, where he engaged in farming and mercantile pursuits. They had six children. She died on July 30, 1873. It was said, "[S]he was a lady of rare excellence of character and sweetness of disposition, and admired and loved by every one with whom she came in contact" (Franklyn Howland, *A Brief Genealogical and Biographical History of Arthur Henry, and John Howland and Their Descendants, of the United States and Canada*; and John F. LaBranche and Rita F. Conant, *In Female Worth and Elegance: Sampler and Needlework Students and Teachers in Portsmouth, New Hampshire, 1741–1840*).

Silk on linen ground of 34 x 29 threads per in.; 17 1/4 in. x 17 3/16 in. Stitches: cross.
1994-179

Figure 54. Sampler by Mercy Hopkins, age eleven, dated 1800; attributed to Burlington County, New Jersey. This sampler is closely related to one worked by Charlotte Hough of Burlington County and inscribed with the school teacher's name, Sarah Shoemaker. The wide-eyed stag, bold sawtooth band, pine trees, hearts, and border of queen's stitch strawberries and flowers are present on both samplers. Charlotte Hough's sampler is illustrated in Ring, *Girlhood Embroidery*, vol. 2, p. 468. I am indebted to Joanne Harvey for bringing to my attention the similarities between these two samplers.

Silk on linen ground of 27 x 27 threads per in.; 13 3/4 in. x 16 1/4 in. Stitches: cross, double cross, drawn work, eyelet, four-sided, outline, queen's, satin.
G1992-149; Anonymous gift in memory of Suzanne S. Flinn

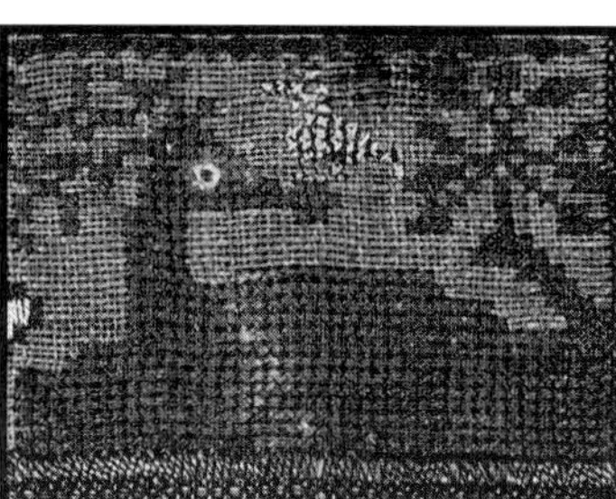

Figure 54A. Mercy Hopkins's wide-eyed stag.

Figure 55. Sampler by Nancey Semple, dated 1798; mid-Atlantic states. Nancey's is one of the earliest of a regional sampler style worked in Maryland, Delaware, and other mid-Atlantic states (my thanks to Deborah Kraak for additional information). Made as late as 1832, examples in this group are distinguished by their realistically worked floral sprays and birds. Some have a center area of alphabets and pious verse separated by an inner border. It is not known whether these designs were the result of the influence of one or several school teachers. For illustrations of related samplers, see Amy Finkel and Morris Finkel, *Samplings: A Selected Offering of Antique Samplers and Needlework* 10, p. 3; and *European and American Furniture and Decorative Arts and Silver*, p. 8, lot 3032.

Silk on linen ground of 38 by 34 threads per in.; 14 1/8 in. x 15 5/8 in. Stitches: chain, cross, eyelet, outline, satin.
1992-10

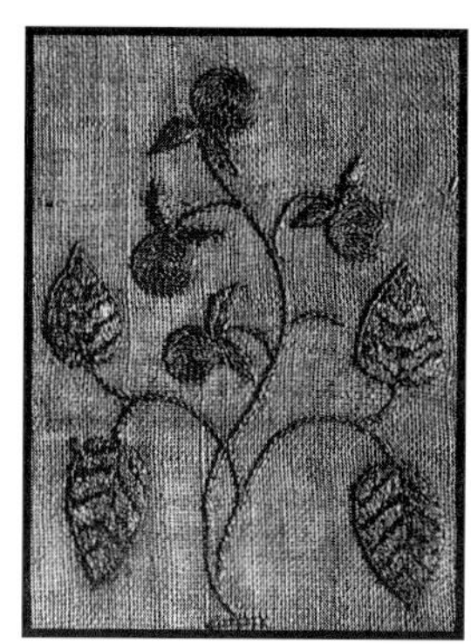

Figure 55A. Strawberry motif from Nancey Semple's sampler.

Figure 56. Sampler by Margaret Williams, dated 1817; "East Nottingham Coecil County State of Maryland." The outer border of realistic floral sprays and inner section of alphabets and pious verse are also seen on Nancey Semple's sampler in figure 55.

Silk on linen ground of 31 x 35 threads per in.; 15 7/8 in. x 16 3/4 in. Stitches: bullion knots, cross, double cross, French knots, eyelet, hem, herringbone, outline, queen's, satin.
1997-2

The District of Columbia

One area that deserves special attention is the District of Columbia.[14] In the famous compromise of 1790, Congress created the District of Columbia from sections of Maryland and Virginia just below the Potomac River fall line. The area, a ten-mile square diamond, was laid out on a north and south axis with the town of Alexandria, Virginia, at its southern tip. In the center of the diamond, next to Georgetown, the federal city was planned. It came to be known as Washington City.[15]

Georgetown

Georgetown was a well-established Maryland tobacco port by the time the District was formed. In addition to the finest shops and inns, it offered the best schools. The reminiscence of a former student tells us how Washington children traveled to school there: "In very bad weather we went in a carriage . . . but on good days we thought nothing of the walk."[16] One such establishment was the Female Seminary of Miss Lydia English, who was educated at the Moravian Academy in Lititz, Pennsylvania. Miss English taught in Georgetown for over thirty years.[17] She rewarded students for diligence and attention to studies, perfect attendance, and punctuality. A number of certificates of merit issued at her school have survived (fig. 57).[18]

Figure 56A. Floral spray on Margaret Williams's sampler.

Washington City

The most easily recognized group of samplers from Washington City was worked between 1810 and 1826 (fig. 58). These architectural samplers, known today as the "Navy Yard samplers," exhibit undulating floral borders and red buildings with white-string courses and checkered bases. These features are also found on Philadelphia samplers.[19] The similarities suggest the presence of a Philadelphia teacher or student who was educated there. This possibility is not unlikely, as we know of other Philadelphia teachers who moved south, probably in hopes of better economic prospects. For example, in 1793 Mrs. Simson, formerly of Philadelphia, Charleston, and New York, advertised that she planned to teach in Alexandria

> all kind of needle work in silk and worsted, crowning, darning, and plain work in the neatest manner; reading and spelling grammatically . . . tambour and embroidery, with elegance and taste; she designs the work and executes the drawing without any additional expence to the ladies. . . .[20]

The earliest sampler from this group was worked in 1810 by Julia Ann Crowley, who stitched the words "Washington Navy Yard" below a prominently placed red building (fig. 59). The building has been identified tentatively as a school building at the Navy Yard. This structure probably burned during the invasion by the British in 1814. Three years after completing her first sampler Julia finished a second—this time on a dark ground and inscribed "Washington City" (fig. 60). The daughter of Timothy Crowley, a ship carpenter, Julia lived at "11e near bridge navy yard."[21] Surnames that appear on other samplers from this group were of families who either lived near the Navy Yard or were employed there.[22]

Figure 57. Certificate of Merit for Catharine Elizabeth Miller; watercolor on paper. Catharine's Certificate of Merit reads as follows: "Female Seminary Georgetown D.C. This certifies that Miss Catharine Elizabeth Miller, during the Term ending this day has strictly complied with the regulation for early rising, thereby meriting approbation in the highest degree and ranking in the first grade for punctuality. / July 31st 1850 / L.S. English / Principal.
6 7/8 in. x 8 3/8 in.
AARFAC, 74.305.1

Another sampler worked in Washington City during this time is Ann Carlon's 1812 embroidery "On Virtue" (fig. 61). Ann's sampler has not been associated with a specific Washington school. The open ground, intricate border, variety of stitches, and use of chenille threads, however, are features seen on other documented Washington samplers of this period.[23]

Figure 58. Sampler by Julia O'Brien, dated June 4, 1812; "Washington City." Julia's sampler is one of the largest group of identified Washington samplers, all completed between 1810 and 1826. They are characterized by large undulating floral borders and red buildings with white-string courses and checkered bases. Others from this group include lawns or stepped terraces dotted with people and animals. For an early description of Julia's sampler, see Bolton and Coe, *American Samplers*, p. 202.
For examples of other samplers in this group, see Ring, *Girlhood Embroidery*, vol. 2, pp. 528–531.

Silk on green linen.
Photograph courtesy Skinner's Auction

Figure 59. Sampler by Julia Ann Crowley, age ten, dated February 10, 1810; "Washington Navy Yard." Julia's sampler is the earliest of the Washington Navy Yard group. In the cartouche above the red building she worked her age and birthday. Julia married Thomas Fitten on June 28, 1820. According to a family letter written in 1925, she died at about the age of thirty-three in Norfolk, leaving several children behind. In the same family letter, she is described as "almost a saint a good catholic and everything that was good" (Garrett, "American Samplers," pp. 694–695).

Silk and chenille on linen ground of 30 x 27 threads per in.; 17 3/4 in. x 21 3/8 in. Stitches: buttonhole, chain, cross, double buttonhole, flat, hem, outline, satin, tent.
1991-25

One 1830 Washington City sampler, which depicts a realistic representation of St. Patrick's Church, proved an unusual research challenge (fig. 62). First, the identification of the sampler maker has been difficult because letters at the beginning and end of her first and surname were removed: [ ]lianna [ ]awrenc[ ].[24] At first glance, one would think that this sampler, inscribed "Washington City," was made there and that the church, worked in such detail, is the St. Patrick's Church, founded between 1792 and 1794, located today near 10th and G Streets in Washington, D.C.

However, it is more probable that the church on the sampler is the fourth church of St. Patrick's in

Figure 60. Sampler by Julia Ann Crowley, age thirteen, dated April 14, 1813; "Washington City." Three years after completing her first sampler, Julia finished a second one, the latter on a dark ground and inscribed "Washington City."

Silk and chenille on linen and wool; 18 3/8 in. x 20 1/2 in. Stitches: cross, French knots, satin, stem.

Photograph courtesy Daughters of the American Revolution Museum, 63.11

Figure 61. Sampler by Ann Carlon, dated May 9, 1812; "Washington City." Ann's sampler features a poem entitled "On Virtue."

Silk and chenille on linen ground of 34 x 29 threads per in.; 12 1/4 in. x 16 3/8 in. Stitches: cable chain, chain, coral knot, couched, cross, outline, queen's, satin, tent.

1996-228,A

Baltimore, the oldest existing Catholic congregation in that city (fig. 63). The following description of the building was published for the 150-year anniversary of the congregation:

> The doors were high with rounded arches at the top, as were the windows. . . . Over the windows fronting Market Street were two marble slabs inscribed with quotations from the Scriptures which were clearly visible from the street. On the slab to the left of one facing the church were the words: "In this place I will give peace, saith the Lord of hosts" (Aggeus, 2:10); on the other was written: "Blessed are they that dwell in Thy house, O Lord" (Psalm, 83:5).[25]

These identical verses flank the steeple in the embroidered sampler. Also represented in stitches is the encircling five-foot brick wall with an iron gate, built in the summer of 1810.

Researchers are not certain if this sampler was actually worked in Washington City, as the inscription would suggest, or if Washington City was the stitcher's hometown. She may have attended St. Patrick's Free School for Girls, which opened in Baltimore in 1815, just across the street from the church.

Figure 63. The fourth St. Patrick's Church; a detail from L.H. Poppleton's *Plan Of The City of Baltimore* (New York, 1823). Marble slabs above the two front windows of the church were inscribed with quotations from the Scriptures: on the left, "In this place I will give peace, saith the Lord of hosts," and on the right, "Blessed are they that dwell in Thy house, O Lord." These same verses appear on the sampler in figure 62.
Photograph courtesy Maryland Historical Society

Figure 62. Sampler by [ ]lianna [ ]awrenc[ ], dated 1830; "Washington City." The fourth St. Patrick's Church in Baltimore was the model for the building embroidered on this sampler. It is not known if the sampler was worked in Washington City. Stylistically this piece is more closely related to the "Baltimore building samplers" than to those known to have been made in Washington City. Another example depicting St. Patrick's Church was worked by Mary Ann Craft of Baltimore in 1822 (Garrett, "American Samplers," p. 699, fig. 10).
Silk on linen ground of 29 x 32 threads per in.; framed size 21 1/4 in. x 22 in. Stitches: cross, outline.
1996-229

Alexandria

At the southern tip of the District of Columbia was the Virginia tobacco port and slave-trading town of Alexandria. It remained part of the District until 1846 when it was returned to Virginia with "great rejoicing and cannon firing."[26] Many advertisements by needlework teachers appeared in Alexandria newspapers during the late eighteenth and early nineteenth centuries. Some of these same teachers also advertised in other Virginia cities. Mrs. Tennant, for example, promoted her tambour school in Norfolk in 1796 and in Alexandria in 1797:

> Mrs. Tennant respectfully informs the ladies of Alexandria that she has opened a school for the purpose of teaching young ladies embroidery, tambouring, open and needle work, flowering, sewing, marking, and spelling, reading, & writing. . . .[27]

Gloria Seaman Allen has shown that there was ample educational opportunity for Alexandria girls of almost all economic classes.[28] One newspaper advertisement attests to the fact that at least a basic education of reading, arithmetic, and plain sewing was available to those of lesser means. In the fall of 1820, Mr. and Mrs. Winter advertised their school on Duke Street as "Cheap Schooling. For Young Misses and Little Ones." Young misses were instructed in reading, grammar, and writing with particular attention "paid to such whose abilities will entitle them to become complete sempstresses." The little ones were taught "their letters, and to spell as far as necessary to carry them into Reading."[29] Ten years earlier, Mrs. Edmonds had informed the public of her intentions to open a school for young ladies in more advanced needlework instruction:

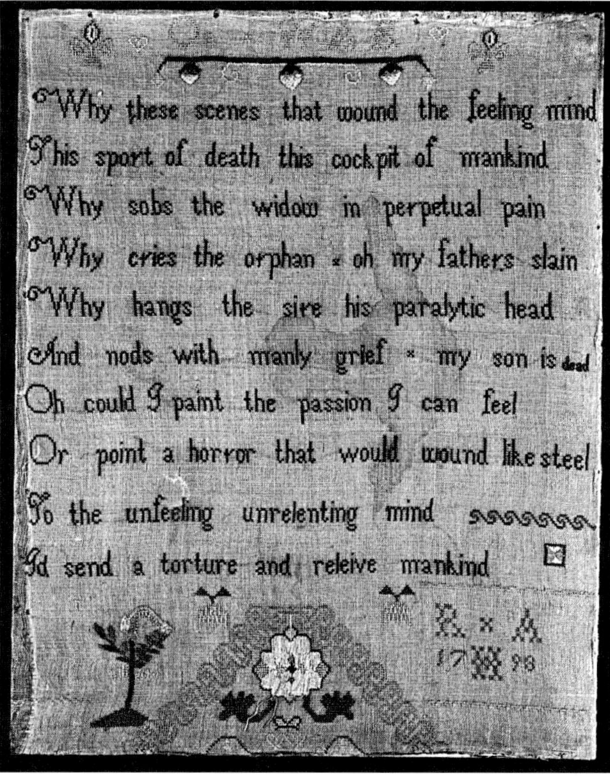

Figure 64. Sampler with poem "On War," attributed to Ann May Horwell, 1798 or later; attributed to Alexandria. The modern viewer cannot help but be caught up in this sampler maker's quiet protest of war, an embroidered declaration that transcends time and speaks to us today. During the Federal period poetry was an acceptable method of expressing emotions. By stitching these words of grief on her sampler, the maker has "painted the passion that she feels."

Silk on linen ground of 34 x 34 threads per in.; 17 in. x 21 3/4 in. Stitches: cross, double cross, eyelet, outline, queen's, satin.
1985-90

Drawing, painting in inks and colors, on satin, tiffany. . . . Embroidery in chenilles, gold, silver and silk. Maps wrought in d[itt]o. Print work in figures or landscapes. Tambour, and Needle work, plain and fanciful. Fringe, and Netting in all its variety. . . .[30]

Despite the many wonderful descriptions of needlework instruction, relatively few samplers made in Alexandria during this time have survived. One Alexandria sampler, along with another not illustrated here, descended in the Horwell family; both were believed to have been worked by Ann May Horwell (fig. 64).[31] The initials R and A above an H, which appear in the right bottom corner of the sampler, were originally thought to stand for Ann May and Richard Horwell, who married in 1810.

Figure 66. Sampler by Marian Wood, dated May 13, 1818; "Alexandria."

Silk on linen ground of 32 x 33 threads per in.; 17 in. x 17 3/16 in. Stitches: cross, queen's.

1995-86; Funded in part by donations from Jeannine's Sampler Seminar

Figure 65. Sampler by Mary Harrison, dated July 1830; "Alexandria."

Silk on linen ground of 29 x 31 threads per in.; 16 5/8 in. x 19 1/2 in. Stitches: chain, cross, double cross, four-sided, outline, queen's.

Photograph courtesy Smithsonian Institution, National Museum of American History, T.147.10

Yet the sampler is dated twelve years earlier. Did an earlier family member work the sampler? Did Ann May work the sampler in 1798 and add the initials after her marriage? Did she complete it after her marriage to commemorate an event that took place in 1798? By learning more about the sampler verse "On War," we hope to answer some of these questions.

The most elaborate group of Alexandria embroideries consists of four samplers worked between 1818 and 1830. They are characterized by beautifully worked strawberry borders in queen's stitch and a prominent columned, two-storied building with flanking rows of trees (figs. 65 and 66). Two of these samplers also feature cornucopias filled with flowers (fig. 67). Illustrated here are three of these samplers. The fourth is known only from a 1921 entry in *American Samplers*. The authors describe an Alexandria sampler worked by Ann Carson and dated July 1818. It features a strawberry border, colonial house, and two cornucopias filled with flowers.[32] Despite numerous hours of research, the school teacher—or teachers—responsible for the designs of these samplers is still in question.[33]

Figure 67. Sampler by Mary Muir, dated June 8, 1818; "Alexandria."

Silk on linen ground of 29 x 35 threads per in.; 17 1/4 in. x 25 1/2 in. Stitches: buttonhole, cross, four-sided, queen's, satin, seed.

Photograph courtesy The Lyceum, Alexandria's History Museum; Purchased in tribute to Mr. and Mrs. Harry A. Councilor, 1986.4.1

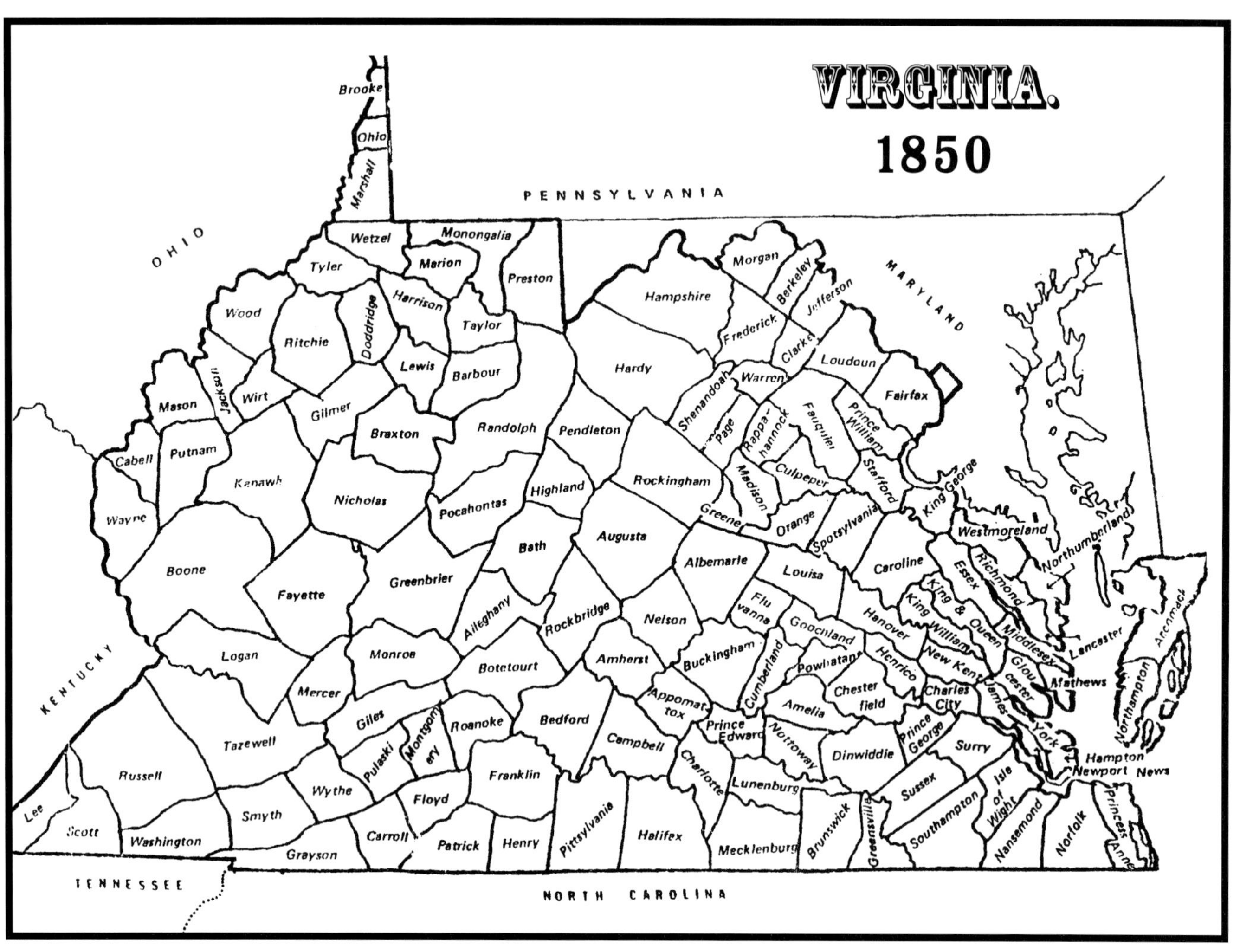

Figure 68. Map of Virginia in 1850, showing county boundaries of the time.
Courtesy of Iberian Publishing Company, Athens, Georgia

FOUR

"In the neatest manner": Virginia Samplers

UNTIL RECENTLY, documented Virginia samplers were rare, and, like other Southern decorative art forms, few were thought to exist (fig. 69). Over the years many reasons for the apparent scarcity of surviving Virginia needlework have been proposed, ranging from climate to loss through war. One might even be tempted to believe the complaint of Captain Alexander Spotswood Dandridge, a Virginia officer in the Revolutionary War. His visit in 1778 to the home of Sally Wister, a young Philadelphia girl, prompted Sally to record the event in her diary. After viewing her sampler "which was in full view" in the parlor, Dandridge remarked that he wished Sally "would teach the Virginians some of [her] needle wisdom; they were the laziest girls in the world."[1]

It has been suggested that the rural environment created by the plantation system, as opposed to the more urban centers in the North, discouraged the establishment and maintenance of needlework schools and teachers.[2] Although a Maryland reference, the letters of Rosalie Steir Calvert, who was introduced in chapter one, are germane to the subject of girlhood education in Virginia. Mrs. Calvert described her thoughts concerning the education of her children when she wrote to her family in Belgium in 1804: "Education for girls is usually very poor, but a mother attentive to her family's interest can easily remedy that, especially in the countryside." Four years later, the education of her children was still of paramount concern, as another letter addressed to her family indicates:

> The best schools for girls here are run by the French. Caroline [age eight] still hasn't been to school. I am teaching her to read and write myself, along with George [age five], but I am about at the point of hiring a tutor, if I can find a suitable one. It will be better than sending them so far away.[3]

Figure 69. Sampler by Sarah H. Buckner, age eleven, dated 1834; attributed to Spotsylvania County, Virginia. Sarah H. Buckner was the daughter of Colonel Richard Buckner of Spotsylvania County.

Silk on linen ground of 29 x 31 threads per in.; 17 5/8 in. x 19 5/8 in. Stitches: cross, eyelet, herringbone, queen's, satin. *1984-10*

Well-to-do Virginia girls were often taught at home by male tutors hired primarily to teach their brothers. In some instances families jointly hired schoolmasters or took advantage of traveling teachers, who offered instruction in such specialized subjects as dance, music, and French.[4] Less fortunate girls relied on their parents, older siblings, and other family members for whatever education they

Figure 70. Sampler, "Lexington Female Academy," dated March 2[8], 1819; Rockbridge County, Virginia. Although the maker of this fragile sampler did not stitch her own name, she did tell us that her sampler was made at Lexington Female Academy. The Presbyterian academy opened in 1807 and operated as a private institution until 1908.

Silk on linen ground of 29 x 27 threads per in.; 17 1/2 in. x 16 1/8 in. Stitches: cross, double cross, eyelet, four-sided.
G1984-149; Gift of Sumpter T. Priddy III

received. Under this kind of educational system it is difficult to identify groups of samplers worked under the direction of one teacher.

Yet Betty Ring tells us that the advertisements for girls' schools that appeared in the colonial papers of Charleston, South Carolina, and Williamsburg, Virginia, rivaled in number the newspaper notices run by teachers in Boston and Philadelphia from the same period. Just as in the North, Southern teachers offered a variety of needlework subjects.[5] For example, in 1770 Patrick Thomas Duke advertised his school in Williamsburg, where he taught "ENGLISH, WRITING, and ACCOUNTS in the best manner." His wife would "likewise teach NEEDLEWORK in the neatest manner."[6] If the success of these schools were to be measured by the number of surviving colonial Virginia samplers, they failed as compared to the number of extant Northern examples.[7] What was the attendance of students at these Southern schools? And where is the needlework that surely must have been made there?

One reason for the sparseness of Virginia examples is the area's hot, humid climate, which certainly is not favorable to the working or survival of needlework. A colonial-period Williamsburg source summarizes the manifest difficulties of stitching needlework in the warm, muggy weather. In August 1769 Anne Blair wrote to her sister about her ten-year-old niece, Betsey Braxton, who was staying with Anne for the summer: "She has finish'd her work'd tucker, but the weather is so warm, that with all the pain's I can take with clean hands, and so forth she cannot help dirtying it a little."[8] In addition, many samplers have survived in poor condition, with missing embroidery threads and deteriorated ground fabric (fig. 70). A few are merely fragments of their original form, complicating their identification (fig. 87).

Some Virginia samplers may be masquerading as English or Scottish examples. A number of early Virginia embroideries bear close similarities to British pieces; a few actually were mistaken for English work until further research was conducted.[9] The precise needlework of the Virginia examples—most notably in the use of reversible stitches—as well as the presence of crowns and Scottish surnames have contributed to this problem. Only the biographical information the needleworker stitched onto some of these examples firmly documents them as Virginian and not English. It is hoped that a combination of genealogical research and close examination of the embroidery techniques will bring more Virginia samplers to light.

Some pieces of needlework are known to have been the casualties of war, stolen by Northern soldiers as they plundered and looted their way through the South. One such example is a sampler begun in 1793 by Martha Carter Fitzhugh of Chatham in Stafford County.[10] Martha Fitzhugh embroidered a family register, recording family births, deaths, and marriages. She died at age seven before finishing it. Her work was completed by a family member, who added Martha's birth and death dates as well as a poem in her memory:

> Her Name shall live and yield a sweet Perfume
> And (tho in Dust) her Memory shall bloom.
> Tho I deplore my Loss and wish it Less,
> Yet will I kiss the Rod and acquiesce.

Eventually the sampler passed into the possession of Martha's niece, Mrs. Robert E. Lee, wife of the Confederate general. It was presumed stolen when Union troops captured Arlington House in 1861. In 1897 the embroidery was recognized at the World's Fair "in a case containing relics exhibited by the Essex Institute in Salem, Massachusetts." Douglas H. Thomas, then editor of the *Virginia Historical Magazine*, wrote, "This sampler was no Doubt 'obtained' during the war by some of the 'visitors' to Virginia, and if publication is made of the fact, it is possible the owner might be found."[11] In 1979 the Essex Institute returned Martha Fitzhugh's work to Arlington House.[12]

Indeed, the South in general suffered far greater losses as a result of the Revolutionary War than did the North, as pointed out by Mary Beth Norton in *Liberty's Daughters: The Revolutionary Experience of American Women, 1750–1800*. By the mid 1780s, Northern cities had largely recovered from the impact of the war and were able to invest both time and money in female academies. This was not true in many Southern towns, where capital was first needed to replace slaves, buildings, and livestock. Norton suggests that in the last two decades of the eighteenth century, wealthy Southern girls wanting an advanced education had to be sent away to boarding schools. One Virginia girl complained of the situation in 1785: "My prospect for a tolerable education is but a bad one, which in my opinion is one of the greatest disadvantages which the Virginia Girls are attended with."[13]

In 1818 Thomas Jefferson wrote to fellow Virginian Nathaniel Burwell about the education of Jefferson's daughters:

> Considering that they would be placed in a country situation where little aid could be obtained from abroad, I thought it essential to give them a solid education, which might enable them, when become mothers, to educate their own daughters, and even to direct the course for sons, should their fathers be lost, or incapable, or inattentive. . . .[14]

It is significant to note that Jefferson's daughter Martha received an education not only out of state but out of the country. In November of 1783, Martha was in Annapolis when her father advised her on how to distribute her time:

> From 8 to 10, practice music.
> From 10 to 1, dance one day and draw another.
> From 1 to 2, draw on the day you dance, and write a letter the next day.
> From 3 to 4, read French.
> From 4 to 5, exercise yourself in music.
> From 5 to bed-time, read English, write, etc.[15]

Four years later, when Martha was enrolled in a French convent, her father, then living in France, wrote to her:

> In the country life of America there are many moments when a women can have recourse to nothing but her needle for employment. In a dull company and in dull weather for instance . . . [t]he needle is then a valuable resource. Besides without knowing to use it herself, how can the mistress of a family direct the works of her servants?[16]

Martha was quick to respond to her father:

> As for needlework, the only kind that I could learn here would be embroidery, indeed netting also; but I could not do much of those in America, because of the impossibility of having proper silks; however, they will not be totally useless.[17]

Other Virginia daughters were sent out of state to school. For example, in January 1793, Frances Thacker Burwell, daughter of Major Nathaniel and Martha Diggs Burwell of King William County, entered the Moravian Seminary in Bethlehem, Pennsylvania.[18] Between 1821 and 1829, three girls from Norfolk and Richmond attended Sarah Pierce's Litchfield Female Academy in Connecticut.[19] Even more notable are the twenty-seven Virginia girls who attended Westtown Boarding School in Chester County, Pennsylvania, between 1799 and 1838.[20]

It is clear from period documents, however, that Virginia girls were working samplers and other embroideries closer to home. As previously mentioned, newspapers contain numerous advertisements by needlework teachers.[21] Stores advertised and sold the necessary materials, and surviving letters and journals describe the embroideries of girls and young women.[22]

Eliza Parke Custis, eldest child of John Parke Custis, tells us something of her childhood education and needlework schedule in a self-portrait of 1808:

> My father in law [step father] willed to give us every advantage, & procured an Instructor to teach us Music, & other branches of Education—the first day he gave me the dedication of the Spectator to read & I heard Dr S tell him "that was an extraordinary child & would if a Boy, make a brilliant figure"—I told them to teach me what they pleased, & observed to them I thought it hard they would not teach me Greek & Latin because I was a girl—they laughed & said women ought not to know those things, & mending, writing, Arithmetic, & Music was all I could be permitted to acquire, I thought of this—with deep regret & began to despise those acquirements which were considered inferior to the others. . . . Patty & I were kept very strictly, when released from Tracy [the tutor] we were obliged to do a certain portion of needlework, & often compelled to practice Lessons of Music . . . we had one pleasure of going two days every week to the dancing school.[23]

Figure 71. View of Hillsborough. Hillsborough overlooks the Mattaponi River in King and Queen County and is the dwelling of Hill family descendants.

One gentry teenager, Frances Baylor Hill of Hillsborough in King William County, described her many needlework activities in a diary she kept from January 1 to December 31, 1797. Although very little is actually known about Frances, her diary captures a year in the life of an intelligent and sensitive girl who described herself and family with frankness and charm. Still occupied by Hill descendants today, Hillsborough stands on a bluff looking out over the

Mattaponi River near Walkerton, Virginia (fig. 71).

Frances began her diary: "Having a bad memory I write this journal that I may with pleasure at the end of the year know who & what I have seen, where I have been & what I have been employ'd about, &c&c." Frances spent most of her days (234 to be exact, but never Sundays) performing some sort of handwork. Her projects ranged from plain sewing—mending, darning, and altering that girls of all social classes needed to know—to the more decorative, or fancy, needlework that was expected of wealthier girls with more leisure time. Entries such as "drew a patron [pattern] and work'd a handkerchief," "knit a little on my stocking," "finish'd my pincushion," and "I work'd a great many leaves on my counterpain [bed covering]" arouse the curiosity of modern readers as we try to visualize the finished projects. Frances's triumphant final entry, written on Sunday, December 31, 1797, provides a colorful glimpse into her personality: "I finish'd my Counterpain on Saturday which has been about 3 year; And now make a conclusion of my journal which has been rather more tedious than I suppos'd it would have been when I first began."[24] That it took Frances only three years to complete her counterpane is remarkable, considering her many other needlework activities during this same period.

Colonial Virginia Samplers

In the 1740s, at a time when American sampler styles were diverging from their English counterparts and regional characteristics were beginning to develop, colonial Virginia needleworkers continued to use the reversible stitches so popular in seventeenth- and very early eighteenth-century English samplers (figs. 72 and 72A). In fact, so fashionable was the English style that needlework teachers in Williamsburg and other Virginia towns often advertised as being "just from England" or "teaching in the English style." The labor-intensive craftsmanship seen in colonial Virginia samplers is paralleled in eastern Virginia furniture of the same period.[25] Colonial Virginians favored the "neat and plain," a style characterized by attention to construction techniques, detail, and finishing rather than showy ornamentation. As a result most early Virginia samplers are understated, beautifully executed works of art.

The earliest identified Virginia sampler to date was made in 1742 by Mary Johnson of New Kent County (fig. 73).[26] However, a sketchy allusion to an earlier family record sampler probably made in 1734 does exist.[27] At first glance, Mary's sampler of alphabets, numbers, and verses appears rather plain and insignificant. However, a closer inspection reveals a combination of certain techniques and motifs that typify Virginia needlework. Mary worked her sampler almost entirely in the marking cross stitch, which creates a back just as finished as the front (figs. 73A and 73B). The only other stitch she used was the Irish stitch, which is rarely found on English and American samplers of the seventeenth and eighteenth centuries but consistently seen on those made in Virginia. The single crown motif is also a feature of later Virginia embroideries. Mary stitched the name Anne Ham[l]in in the bottom right corner. Could this possibly have been her needlework instructor? If so, in addition to being the earliest recognized Virginia sampler, Mary's work would be the earliest to include a teacher's name. This has yet to be confirmed.

The same combination of motifs and techniques appears in an unfinished sampler from Isle of Wight County made by Sellah Fulgham in 1761 (fig. 74). Sellah's stitches are so neatly executed that the back of her work mirrors its front. The crowns and zigzag area of Irish stitch in the bottom left corner are familiar features of Virginia samplers (fig. 74A). The inscription is a variation of a then-popular

Figure 72. Reverse side of sampler by Rebekah Osbourne, dated 1728; attributed to England. Shown from the back, Rebekah Osbourne's sampler is typical in shape and design of both English and American examples in the first three decades of the eighteenth century. It is worked in reversible stitches, creating an extremely neat back. This characteristic continues to be seen on Virginia samplers throughout the eighteenth and into the early nineteenth centuries.

Silk on linen ground of 38 x 38 threads per in.; 9 1/4 in. x 17 3/4 in. Stitches: back, cross, eyelet, hem, marking cross, satin, tent.
1950-154

Figure 72A. Detail of reverse side of Rebekah Osbourne's work.

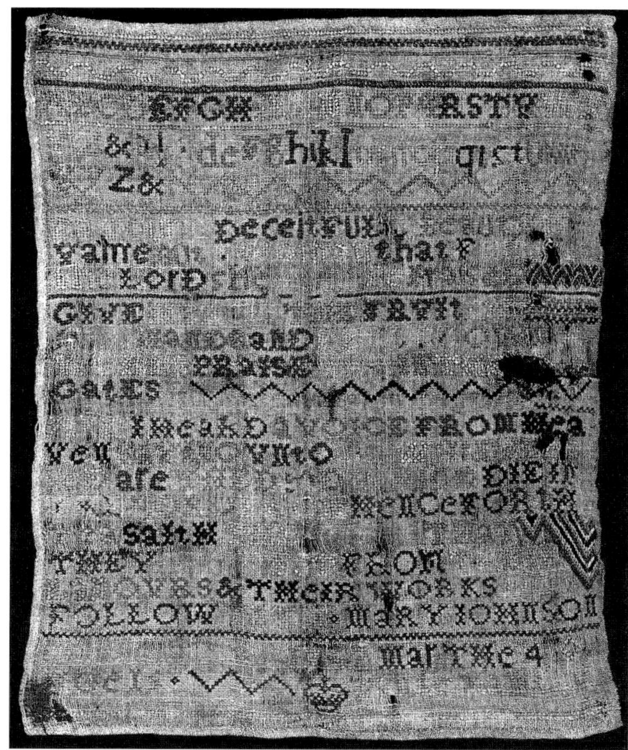

Figure 73. Sampler by Mary Johnson, age twelve, dated 1742; attributed to the Chesapeake region of Virginia. Mary's work is the earliest-dated Virginia sampler.

Silk on linen ground of 38 x 34 threads per in.; 9 in. x 10 3/4 in. Stitches: Irish, marking cross.
1987-716,1

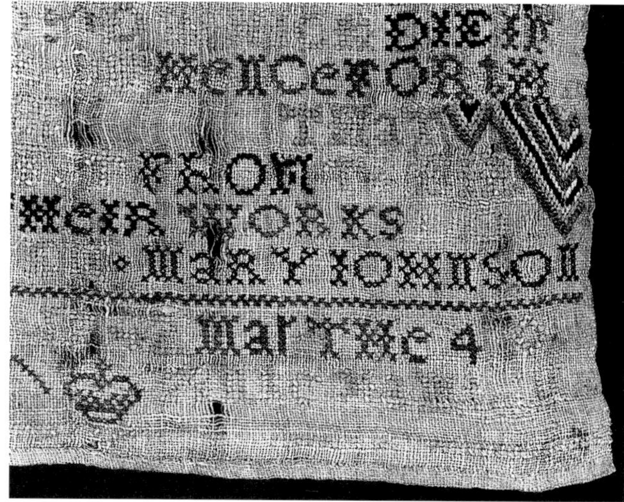

Figure 73A. Detail of front of Mary Johnson's work.

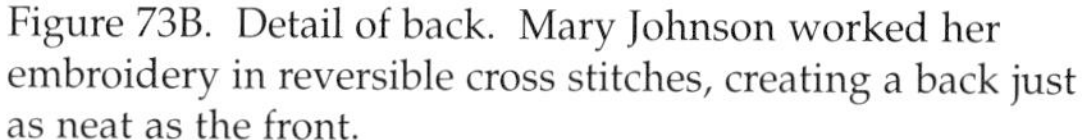

Figure 73B. Detail of back. Mary Johnson worked her embroidery in reversible cross stitches, creating a back just as neat as the front.

Figure 74. Sampler by Sellah Fulgham, dated May 20, 1761; Isle of Wight County, Virginia. Sellah's stitches are so neatly executed that the back of her sampler mirrors its front.

Silk on linen ground of 40 x 31 threads per in.; 8 7/8 in. x 18 1/8 in. Stitches: double cross, eyelet, herringbone, Irish, marking cross, satin.

G1988-460; Gift from the estate of Mary Wrenn Cofer Ballard in honor of her daughters, Mary Wrenn Ballard Oliver and Anne Lewis Ballard Weaver

Figure 74A. Detail of Sellah Fulgham's sampler. The crowns and zigzag area of Irish stitch in the left bottom corner are also features that distinguish Virginia samplers.

Figure 75. Sampler by Mary Ambler, ca. 1770; attributed to Yorktown or Williamsburg, Virginia.
Silk on linen ground of 22 x 25 threads per in.; 6 3/8 in. x 10 3/4 in. Stitches: eyelet, four-sided, marking cross.
John Marshall House, Association for the Preservation of Virginia Antiquities

Figure 76. Reverse side of Mary Ambler's sampler. The back view of Mary's sampler shows that she worked it entirely in reversible stitches.
John Marshall House, Association for the Preservation of Virginia Antiquities

Figure 77. Portrait of Mary Ambler Marshall, by unknown artist. Crayon (pastel) on parchment; Richmond, Virginia; 16 3/4 in. x 21 in. Inscribed in ink on the back of this drawn portrait is "Mary Ambler Marshall/Richmond, Va. / 1799."
Photograph courtesy Museum of Early Southern Decorative Arts; Gift of G. Wilson Douglas, Jr.

verse: "Sellah Fulgham is My Name Virginia is / My Nation the Isle White My Dwelling Place / And Christ My Salvation May the 20th / 1761 Worked this Samplar."

Another colonial sampler characterized by its neat back was worked by Mary Ambler (figs. 75 and 76). Mary Willis Ambler Marshall, born in 1761, was the daughter of Jaquelin Ambler of Yorktown and Rebecca Burwell of Carter's Grove. Mary's father played an important role in the education of his family. In 1857, historian Bishop William Meade wrote of the family:

> Her mother being in very bad health, her father . . . devoted all his spare hours to the education of herself [Mary's sister] and her sister, (afterwards Mrs. Marshall), then only five or six years of age. The copies for writing were always written by himself, in a fair hand, containing some moral or religious sentiment, but defective in grammar, that they might correct them; and so of other branches. The advantages they possessed were superior to any enjoyed in those days, when there were no boarding-schools and all that was taught "was reading and writing, at twenty shillings a year and a load of wood."[28]

Mary's sampler is proof, however, that in addition to her father's instruction, she received some type of formal education outside the home. Familiarly known as "Polly," she married John Marshall, the future chief justice of the United States Supreme Court, in 1783 and lived in Richmond until her death in 1831 (fig. 77).

Elizabeth Richards's sampler is one of the few colonial Virginia samplers not worked in the marking stitch (fig. 78). However, she did use other reversible stitches, such as eyelet and four-sided, to create a neat back. The clue that led to the identification of Elizabeth as the maker was the name "Mrs. Daniel Triplett" penciled on cardboard on the back of the piece. Elizabeth was the daughter of English-born John Richards and Susannah Coleman of Stafford County, Virginia. She married Daniel Triplett, one of the "gentlemen justices" of Stafford County, in 1774. Together they had at least six children. Elizabeth died in Norfolk on September 24, 1826.[29]

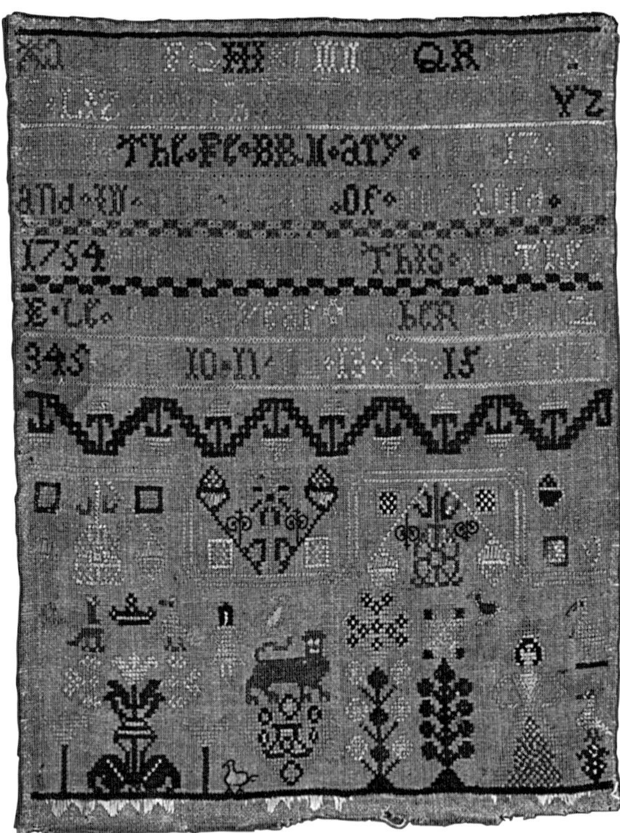

Figure 78. Sampler by Elizabeth Richards, age ten, dated 1764; attributed to the Chesapeake region of Virginia.
Silk on linen ground of 41 x 35 threads per in.; 8 1/2 in. x 11 in. Stitches: cross, double cross, four-sided, eyelet, herringbone, satin.
1991-161

Figure 79. "The Sacrifice of Isaac" by Elizabeth Boush, age sixteen, dated 1768–1769; Norfolk, Virginia. Elizabeth's picture may have been the last of a series of needlework projects—her first being a sampler—that she worked under the watchful direction of her needlework teacher, Mrs. Elizabeth Gardiner Armston.

Silk on silk ground of 38 x 40 threads per in.; 11 1/2 in. x 19 1/2 in. Stitches: tent.

Museum of Early Southern Decorative Arts, Gift of Mrs. James H. Stone

Figure 80. "Sacrifice of Isaac," maker unknown, ca. 1650; England. The story represented here is from the book of Genesis, chapter 22. Abraham is ordered by God to sacrifice his own son, Isaac. As Abraham and Isaac prepare to carry out God's will, however, an angel appears and stops the proceedings. This is a story of faith and obedience. Did the young needleworkers learn this lesson as they patiently stitched their silk embroideries?

Silk on linen ground of 54 x 56 threads per in.; framed size 11 1/4 in. x 15 in. Stitches: French knot, tent.

1962-107

Figure 81. Portrait of Elizabeth Boush by John Durand, 1769; Norfolk, Virginia. Oil on canvas; 25 1/2 in. x 30 in. Elizabeth Boush (born 1753), a member of an old and established Norfolk family, was sixteen years old when she sat for this portrait. Three years after the painting was completed Elizabeth married Champion Travis of Jamestown Island ("Travis Family," p. 143; Mrs. Russell S. Barrett, "Marriage Bonds of Norfolk County," p. 108). Following his active service in the Revolution, the couple moved to Williamsburg, eventually residing in the frame house that stands across Francis Street from the Public Hospital. They had seven children. Susan Travis, their sixth child, married Edmund Ruffin, renowned for allegedly firing the first shot against Fort Sumter (*Dictionary of American Biography*, vol. 3, pp. 214–216; I am indebted to Martha R. Jones for bringing this to my attention).
1982-271

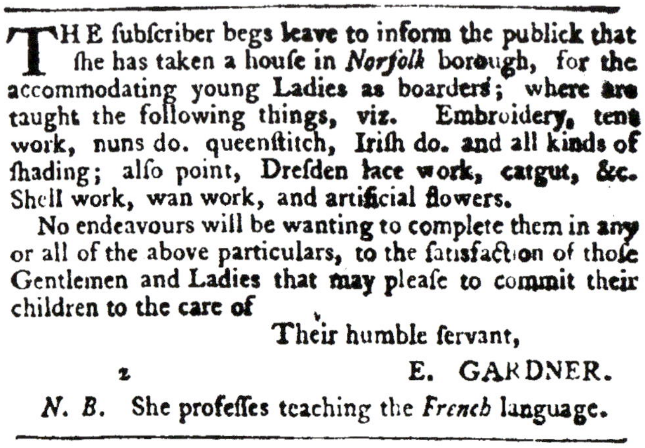

Before leaving the colonial period, an extraordinary Virginia embroidery deserves attention. Between 1768 and 1769, Elizabeth Boush of Norfolk worked a rare silk embroidered picture (fig. 79). The exquisite craftsmanship in the shading of this piece is yet another example of the skill seen in early Virginia needlework. The subject matter of Elizabeth's embroidery, "Sacrifice of Isaac," was probably derived from a block print in the *Thesaurus Sacrarum Historiarum Veteris Testament*, published by Gerard de Jode in Antwerp in 1585.[30] This volume, as well as other engravings and woodcuts, remained an important design source for needlework for three centuries. Old Testament subjects in particular were popular with English schoolgirls throughout the seventeenth and eighteenth centuries, and by the early 1700s, with American schoolgirls as well (fig. 80).

Betty Ring was the first scholar to recognize the significance of this embroidery: it is the earliest identified American needlework picture to name a teacher. Moreover, it is the only colonial Virginia needlework known to have been made at a specific school. The embroidered inscription beneath the silk needlework reads, "Elizth Boush Workd this Piece at E. Gardners 1768 9."

THE ſubſcriber begs leave to inform the publick that ſhe has taken a houſe in *Norfolk* borough, for the accommodating young Ladies as boarders; where are taught the following things, viz. Embroidery, tent work, nuns do. queenſtitch, Iriſh do. and all kinds of ſhading; alſo point, Dreſden lace work, catgut, &c. Shell work, wan work, and artificial flowers.

No endeavours will be wanting to complete them in any or all of the above particulars, to the ſatisfaction of thoſe Gentlemen and Ladies that may pleaſe to commit their children to the care of

Their humble ſervant,
E. GARDNER.

N. B. She profeſſes teaching the *French* language.

Figure 82. Newspaper advertisement from the *Virginia Gazette*, Williamsburg, March 21, 1766. *Courtesy Virginia Historical Society*

Elizabeth Gardner Armston, the E. Gardner noted in the inscription, advertised her Norfolk school in the *Virginia Gazette* from 1766 until 1772 (fig. 82). Little is known about her before her marriage to Freer Armston, an English merchant and soap-boiler, on November 25, 1769. Armston ran a notice in the *Virginia Gazette* in March 1774 : "The Subscriber intending to leave the Colony for a few months, requests the favour of those indebted to him to settle their Accounts immediately."[31] Shortly thereafter, in 1775, the Armstons, who were loyalists, sought refuge with Lord Dunmore and the British fleet. This must have been a difficult time, as Elizabeth was "then Big with Child," in addition to having a fourteen-month-old daughter. After enduring much hardship, the Armstons finally reached England in 1777. They claimed financial losses in Virginia of £1,001.[32]

Elizabeth Boush completed her needlework picture the same year she sat for a portrait (fig. 81). Although the flowers in Elizabeth's hair and on her gown are stylistic conventions often used by artists of the period, the garland of artificial flowers she holds may be an example of her own handiwork. The skill of artificial flowers was taught at E. Gardner Armston's school.

Eighteenth-Century Virginia Samplers

Four eighteenth-century samplers, probably from King William County, were worked by a mother and her two daughters. The mother, Barbara Fox, included family initials and "Barbara Fox Was born July 9 1752" on her alphabet sampler, worked in cross and eyelet stitches. Later she married Drury Ragsdale of King William County, Virginia. A graduate of the College of William and Mary, her husband served as a magistrate and a commissioner of peace for King William County. Barbara may have been responsible for the needlework education of

Figure 83. Sampler by Frances Ragsdale, age twelve, dated 1797; attributed to King William County, Virginia.
Silk on linen ground; 12 in. x 13 3/8 in. Stitches: cross, eyelet.
Valentine Museum

Figure 84. Sampler by Mildred Ragsdale, age twelve, dated 1800; attributed to King William County, Virginia.
Silk on linen ground of 23 x 24 threads per in.; 11 1/2 in. x 12 1/4 in. Stitches: cross, eyelet.
Jamestown-Yorktown Educational Trust

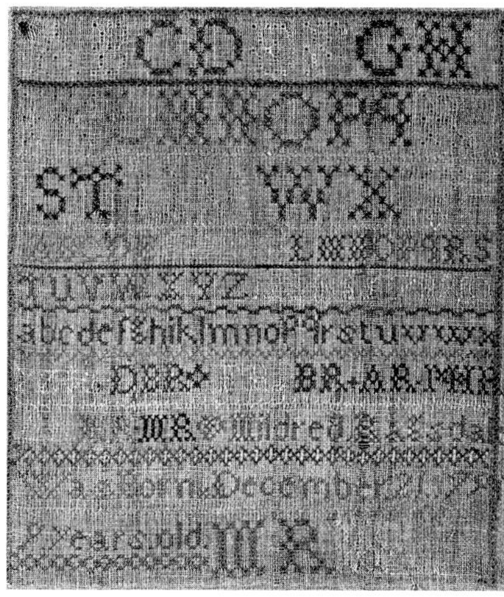

her daughters, Frances and Mildred. Frances worked two simple alphabet samplers in the late eighteenth century (fig. 83). In 1800 the younger daughter, Mildred, also worked an alphabet sampler in cross and eyelet stitches (fig. 84).[33]

Not illustrated here but important to note is another example of a simple alphabet sampler, also stitched in cross and eyelet stitches. It is the work of six-year-old Cornelia Lee, completed in 1786.[34] Cornelia was the daughter of William Lee of Stratford and Hannah Philippa Ludwell of Green Spring in James City County. William Lee was a Virginia merchant who traded in Europe, where Cornelia was not only born but also spent much of her early life. Between the years of her mother's death in 1784 and that of her father in 1795 it is not clear where Cornelia and her older sister, Portia, lived. They could well have resided at Green Spring, where opportunities for education were available in nearby Williamsburg. It is known that after they were orphaned, they stayed with various relatives, including Francis Lightfoot and Rebecca Tayloe Lee at Menokin Plantation on the Rappahannock River. From 1797 to 1806 they lived at Sully in Fairfax County as wards of Richard Bland and Elizabeth Collins Lee.[35]

Williamsburg

By the 1790s we clearly see the results of the development of the distinct regional styles in Virginia samplers that distinguish them from embroideries made in other areas of the new Republic. It is not surprising that at this time the earliest group of identified Virginia schoolgirl embroideries was worked in Williamsburg. From 1699 to 1780, the town served as the capital of the Virginia colony. Perhaps more significantly, it was a cultural and political center, ranking in importance with Boston, Philadelphia, New York, Annapolis, and Charleston.

Figure 85. Sampler by Ann Pasteur Maupin, age ten, dated October 20, 1791; Williamsburg, Virginia. This sampler is worked entirely in reversible stitches. Ann lived in Williamsburg with her parents, Gabriel and Dorcus Maupin. Her father worked as a saddler, harnessmaker, and tavern keeper before he was appointed keeper of the Williamsburg Magazine with the rank of captain, a post he held for sixteen years. Ann married Norborne Booth Beall in Williamsburg on November 30, 1799. In 1800 they moved to Kentucky, where Ann died sometime between 1824 and 1856 (Margie G. Brown, comp., *Genealogical Abstracts: Revolutionary War Veterans Scrip Act 1852*, pp. 336, 337; genealogical notes on the family of Ann Pasteur Maupin and Norborne Booth Beall supplied by family member Howard Singleton in 1981 and 1994).

Silk on linen ground of 32 x 39 threads per in.; 11 1/8 in. x 16 in. Stitches: double cross, eyelet, marking cross, outline, running. *1981-161*

Figure 86. Sampler by Sarah Walker Waller, age eleven, ca. 1791; attributed to Williamsburg, Virginia. Sarah Walker Waller was the daughter of Judith Page and John Waller of Spotsylvania and King William Counties, Virginia. While attending school in Williamsburg, Sarah possibly could have lodged at the home of her aunt and uncle, Catharine Page and Benjamin Carter Waller (George Norbury MacKenzie and Nelson Osbood Rhodes, *Colonial Families of the United States*, pp. 368, 369). (Sarah was the second cousin of Emma Page; see her sampler in figure 9.)

Silk on linen ground of 44 x 45 threads per in.; 18 3/8 in. x 17 in. Stitches: cross, double cross, eyelet, herringbone, satin.
Clark County Historical Association

Figure 86A. Detail of figure 86. These motifs are probably similar to designs on Sarah Hornsby's sampler, current whereabouts unknown, also from Williamsburg and described in Bolton and Coe, *American Samplers*.

Figure 87. Sampler, maker unknown, ca. 1791; attributed to Williamsburg, Virginia. Much to our delight this small fragment of a sampler was discovered in a Williamsburg yard sale and brought to our attention. It is missing its bottom quarter, but even without that section we can clearly see how similar this sampler is to the others from Williamsburg.

Silk on linen ground of 41 x 41 threads per in.; 10 3/4 in. x 10 1/8 in. Stitches: cross, eyelet.
G1990-94; Gift of Janet Cook Howard

As early as 1752, John Walker, "LATELY arriv'd in Williamsburg from London," advertised in the *Virginia Gazette* that his wife taught "young ladies all kinds of needlework."[36] In 1776, Mrs. Neill proposed opening a boarding school

> in Williamsburg for the Reception of young Ladies, on the same Plan of the English Schools . . . She will instruct them in Reading, Tambour and other Kinds of Needle Work . . . As Nothing tends more to the Improvement of a Country than proper Schools for the Education of both Sexes.[37]

One wonders if Mrs. Neill's boarding school was the "fashionable boarding school" Helen Maxwell Read (born Norfolk, 1750; died Norfolk, 1833) remembered as she dictated her life story to her son, William Maxwell, in the early nineteenth century:

> I was put to school to a poor old dame by the name of Mrs. Drudge, and, to be sure, she did drudge to teach me my letters—spelling and reading after a fashion. . . . She taught me to read the Bible. . . . After I had learned out here, I was sent to a Mrs. Johnson—a very large fat woman. . . She taught me needle-work, and marking on the sampler . . . my father, who thought me a very fine smart girl (for, I was always his favorite), wished to send me to a fashionable boarding school that there was then in Williamsburg, but my mother would not consent, saying, she could not part with me.[38]

This important Williamsburg group consists of four samplers, three of which are illustrated here, all worked in the last decade of the eighteenth century under the guidance of an anonymous school mistress. The antecedents of this group, however, can be traced to a sampler worked earlier, in 1769, by Mary Powell of Yorktown.[39] Features characteristic of the group include figures of Adam and Eve, the tree of knowledge, serpents, birds, crowns, hearts, tall slender bushes, and bands of waves—worked in very fine cross stitches. Ann Pasteur Maupin, age ten in 1791, stitched her sampler on a thin linen ground using exclusively reversible stitches (fig. 85). Her neatness is not so puzzling when we recall that household linens were often marked with reversible stitches because they were seen from both sides when in use.[40]

Sarah Walker Waller worked a closely related sampler on a similarly fine linen ground with silk embroidery threads (fig. 86). Ann's and Sarah's samplers share several characteristics: tall slender bushes, hearts, swooping birds, and the technique of working the capital letters of each word in different colored silk. The fragment of a third sampler with many of these features is missing the bottom section where the signature line and date would have been worked (fig. 87). However, both the close similarities to the two pieces described previously and its Williamsburg family history leave no doubt that this third fragmentary example was made under the same instructor.

The current whereabouts of a fourth Williamsburg sampler related to the above three embroideries is unknown. However, we know of its existence from an entry in *American Samplers* (fig. 86A). The authors described a Williamsburg sampler made by Sarah Hornsby about 1793, which features related elements: very fine cross stitch; a tree of life; Adam and Eve; a serpent; and isolated figures such as birds, trees, castles, and baskets of flowers. The verse is identical to that on Ann Maupin's sampler: "Oh Heavenly Virtue Thine A Sacred Flame / And still My Soul Pays Homage to Thy Name."[41] Sarah Hornsby presumably worked her sampler with the same schoolmistress who taught Ann Pasteur Maupin, Sarah Walker Waller, and the unidentified maker of the sampler fragment.

A lithograph is of special interest because it depicts the "Williamsburg Female Academy (fig. 88).

Very little is known about the school. The print could be a later rendering of the Williamsburg Female Academy, which two professors at the College of William and Mary advertised as early as 1808. Although it is not known if needlework was part of the curriculum, the notice states that, in addition to a highly academic agenda, female accomplishments were offered:

> WILLIAMSBURG FEMALE ACADEMY. — Mr. Blackburn . . . and Mr. Plunkett . . . inform the public that they have united for the purpose of establishing an Academy in which young Ladies may receive an education, calculated at once, to improve and enlarge the understanding, and to ensure the acquisition of those accomplishments, which are not only extremely agreeable in themselves, but which have become essential requisites in polished societies . . . lessons in Reading, Writing, Arithmetic, English Grammar, Composition, Geography and History. . . . Should any of these young ladies discover a taste and capacity for further scientific acquirements, he will undertake to conduct them through certain Mathematical, Astronomical, and Philosophical branches, . . . On the succeeding day, Mr. Plunkett will teach the French Language, Music, theoretically and practically, Dancing and Drawing.[42]

It is possible that a surviving May 1852 report card for a Miss F. Hurt from the Williamsburg Female Academy was issued from this school or from a later institution that employed the same name.[43]

In contrast to the Williamsburg Female Academy, the Bray School, a charity school for black children, operated in Williamsburg from 1760 until the death of its mistress, Mrs. Anne Wager, in 1774. Funded by a British society called the "Associates of the late Dr. Bray," its main objective was to instruct "Negro Children in the Principles of the Christian Religion." The regulations to be observed by the

Figure 88. Print, *Williamsburg Female Academy*, ca. 1845. Lithograph with watercolor; drawn by W. F. Grabau. Printed by "P. S. Duval's Steam lith Press"; Philadelphia, Pennsylvania. *1930-606*

"tutoress or mistress" stipulated that "she shall teach her female Scholars knitting sewing & such other Things as may be useful to their Owners. . . ."[44] No known needlework survives from this school. Indeed, no known Virginia sampler made by an African-American girl survives. However, one 1807 advertisement from a Norfolk newspaper illuminates the needlework skills of a runaway slave girl. Such proficiency was probably learned at the side of her mistress.

> Ranaway from the subscriber . . . living near the City of Richmond . . . a mulatto girl by the name of Nancy between 17 and 18 . . . has been brought up to the house business, is a good sempstress, can knit, and understands the marking very well by a sampler. . . .[45]

Figure 89. Pinball marked "a trifle from Margare[t]," dated 1782; England. Early pincushions and pinballs were often highly decorated and reflected the high value placed on the pins themselves. This pinball, with its Quaker-like eight-pointed star, tree, and birds, is similar to others made at the Quaker school in Ackworth, England.

Knitted silk with braided cord, 22 stitches per in., 25 rows per in.; approximately 2 in. diameter.
1953-212

Figure 90. Pinball with chain and ring by an unknown maker, dated 180[?8]; attributed to mid-Atlantic states. This pinball is made of two fabric sections sewn together over a stuffed ball cushion. The fabric is worked in tiny cross stitches in geometric patterns and floral sprays, motifs characteristic of Quaker needlework from the Delaware River valley. Stitched under the silver ring is the possible date of 1808. The attached silver ring and chain allow the pinball to hang at a lady's waist from a chatelaine or belt.

Silk on linen ground, silver ring and chain; 7 in. diameter. Stitches: cross, whip.
1996-106,A-B

Quaker Needlework

Regardless of where it was made, Quaker needlework has its own distinctive and uniform characteristics. Quaker women teaching in the North as well as in Virginia used a particular style of lettering and a repertoire of motifs that probably originated at the Friends' Schools in Ackworth and York, England (fig. 89). The Quaker alphabet is distinct in its size, boldness, and plain roman style. The center lines of the letters M and N descend to the baseline, the J and Q often extend below it. Among the typical Quaker motifs, usually worked in cross stitches, are pairs of birds, wreaths, sprays of flowers

Figure 91. Sampler by Martha L. Strode, dated 1817; attributed to mid-Atlantic states. Martha's sampler is enclosed in the popular Westtown undulating vine-and-leaf border with an eight-leaf design at top. Her extract is from *A Treasury of Poems from Worship and Devotion* by Thomas Moore (1779–1852). Although the name Martha L. Strode does not appear in the general catalog of Westtown students, it is probable that she was related to the other Strodes or Strouds who did attend the school.

Silk on linen ground of 58 x 72 threads per in.; 14 in. x 12 1/2 in. Stitches: cross, outline, satin, tent.
1995-9,A

such as roses and lilies of the valley, and geometric medallions or half-medallions (fig. 90). Vine and leaf borders frequently encircle Quaker verses (called "extracts" by the Quakers) and octagonal borders enclose inscriptions such as "An Emblem of Innocence" or "An Emblem of Love" (fig. 91). A distinctive feature found on some Quaker samplers is ligatures, that is, characters containing two or more united letters.

Members of the Society of Friends, the name Quakers gave themselves, conducted their lives according to the principles of equality, simplicity, and peace. These ideals were expressed in two maxims central to Quaker beliefs: "Something of God is borne in every human being" and "All are equal." Such attitudes ensured that Quaker girls had the same opportunities as boys, especially concerning education.

The best-known Quaker school of the early nineteenth century was Westtown Boarding School, established in 1794 by the Society of Friends in Chester County, Pennsylvania. Still in operation today, Westtown received its first students, of both sexes, in 1799. With the exception of sewing, which was unique to the girls' curriculum, Quaker teachers offered all subjects, including reading, writing, arithmetic, and bookkeeping, to girls as well as boys.

Although most of the boarding school's students came from Pennsylvania, Delaware, and New Jersey, some did travel from as far away as New York, Ohio, and North Carolina. Between 1799 and 1838, twenty-seven Virginia girls attended the school.[46] It is amazing that a sampler worked by one of these students—Sarah Ann Lupton of Waterford, Virginia—has survived (fig. 92). In April of 1819, at the age of thirteen, Sarah entered Westtown School, which was a journey of well over 120 miles by horse or carriage from her home in Loudoun County, Virginia. She was just one of a growing population of American girls who lived away from home and family for an extended length of time while obtaining an education. Two other girls from Waterford, Mary Steer and Sarah E. Thompson, were also students at Westtown during this period.[47] The duty felt by their

Figure 92. Sampler by Sara Ann Lupton, age thirteen, dated 1819; "Weston," Chester County, Pennsylvania. Sara Ann Lupton was the daughter of Samuel Lupton of Waterford in Loudoun County, Virginia. She was one of twenty-seven Virginia girls who attended the Westtown School between 1799 and 1838.

Silk on linen ground of 28 x 28 threads per in.; 14 1/2 in. x 16 1/2 in. Stitches: cross. *The Children's Museum of Indianapolis, 67.170*

mothers and fathers to educate them properly outweighed the expense, potential dangers, and pain of separation that parents and daughters must have endured.[48] Certainly the three girls were acquainted with each other. It is hoped that their mutual companionship eased the pain of separation from home and family.

Quaker Samplers Made in Virginia

The first Quaker messenger (the Quaker term for missionary) arrived in Virginia as early as 1655 and was well received in Norfolk, Nansemond, Isle of Wight, and Suffolk Counties. Over the next 120 years numerous Quaker meetings were established

Figure 93. Sampler by Maria Coles, age twelve or thirteen, dated 1808; attributed to Hanover County, Virginia. Maria may have worked her sampler at Cedar Creek Meeting, where a school opened in 1791.

Silk on linen ground of 31 x 33 threads per in.; 17 in. x 16 1/2 in. Stitches: cross.

G1997-14; Gift of Nancy Chappelear Baird

Figures 93A (above) and 93B (below). Details of half-medallions on Maria Coles's sampler.

throughout Virginia. Records indicate that between 1780 and 1810 over 60 different Quaker meetings existed. During this latter period local Friends Meetings established schools all across Virginia, including the towns of Petersburg, Lynchburg, and Waterford. While no period reference has been found to indicate that needlework was a part of the curricula of these schools, surviving Virginia samplers depicting Quaker alphabets and motifs would suggest that this was the case.

Maria Coles's sampler of 1808 is an example of one of those Virginia samplers heavily influenced by Quaker needlework, with its geometric half-medallions and sprigs of flowers (fig. 93).[49] Three of these half-medallions appear on both Maria's and Sara Ann Lupton's samplers (figs. 93A and 93B). Maria Coles was born July 1, 1795, at "Coles Hill" in Hanover County. Her parents, Walter Coles, Jr., and Mary Randolph Price, were members of the Cedar Creek Meeting, which opened a school in 1791.[50] It is believed that Maria attended this Quaker school, where she presumably worked her sampler. On January 23, 1813, she married William Shelton of "Woodlawn," Louisa County, Virginia.[51]

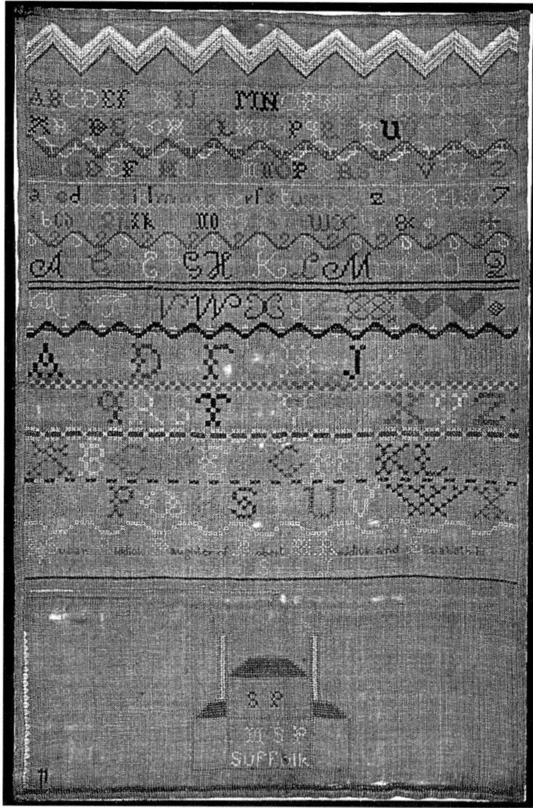

Figure 94. Sampler by Susan Riddick, age fifteen, dated January 31, 1806; "Suffolk," Virginia. Susan's sampler remained in the Prentis family until 1978, when Colonial Williamsburg accessioned it as the first Virginia sampler in the Foundation's collection.

Silk on linen ground of 27 x 23 threads per in.; 16 1/2 in. x 25 in. Stitches: cross, double cross, eyelet, hem, Irish variation, marking cross, queen's.
1978-91

Quaker Samplers South of the James River

Throughout the eighteenth and into the nineteenth century Quaker influence was felt especially in the area south of the James River. A group of four known samplers from this region, three of which are shown here, is characterized by Quaker motifs, identical alphabets, the unusually large size of the embroideries, and pieced ground fabrics.[52] These examples also reflect Virginia sampler features common in the previous century: the use of Irish stitch, or areas worked to resemble Irish stitch, and patterns worked in reversible stitches. The backs of the samplers are extremely neat.

Susan Riddick worked her 1806 sampler, inscribed "Suffolk," predominantly in reversible stitches (fig. 94). The band at the top of her embroidery is a variation of the Irish stitch. Susan Caroline Riddick (born October 6, 1791; died October 19, 1862) was the daughter of Colonel Robert Moore and Elizabeth Riddick Carr Riddick of Nansemond County. Four years after completing her sampler, she married Joseph Prentis II and they made their

Figure 95. *The Monitor's Instructor, or a System of Practical Geography of the United States of America*, by James Iddings; Wilmington: Printed by William Black, 1804. Susan Riddick owned this book of geography lessons. It includes a wonderful description of Williamsburg in "disgrace and ruin" after the capital of Virginia moved to Richmond in 1780.
John D. Rockefeller, Jr. Library, Webb-Prentis Collection (G125.133), Colonial Williamsburg Foundation

home in Suffolk.[53] Susan may have added the initials SP and MSP inside the outlines of the house after her marriage. Or perhaps a daughter made the modification because the stitches appear to have been worked by a different hand. Sewing was not the only lesson that young Susan studied (fig. 95). She signed a geography book she once owned in much the same way that a sampler is inscribed; "Susan Riddick Her Book Suffo. 6th May 1804." She also wrote this charming verse, which she presumably composed herself:

> Susan Riddick
> doth me possess
> I am hers I do confess
> If she me lose & you me find
> I beg my friend you'll be so kind
> As to return me again to her
> And I'll respect you ever after.

Esther Shivers, also of Nansemond County, worked her sampler, dated 1808, with sprays of Quaker-style roses and lilies of the valley and a wreath encircling a bird (fig. 96). The rare dark-colored ground of her sampler is actually two pieces of linen seamed together. The join is embellished with a herringbone border. Both this and the third sampler in the group, worked by Sarah Bruce Butt, have large bands at the top worked in cross stitch to resemble Irish stitch. Sarah's work reflects the Quaker style—the octagonal medallion enclosing a bird and vine and baskets and sprays of flowers (fig. 97). Large areas of her sampler, such as the unidentified house, are worked in marking cross.

Mary A. D. Craddock's work exhibits an area of Irish stitch in its top right corner (fig. 98). The format and size of this piece, plus an identical uppercase script alphabet, suggest that her sampler is associated with this Quaker group. The two figures at the bottom left corner are rarely seen on Virginia needlework, however. Mary also executed a

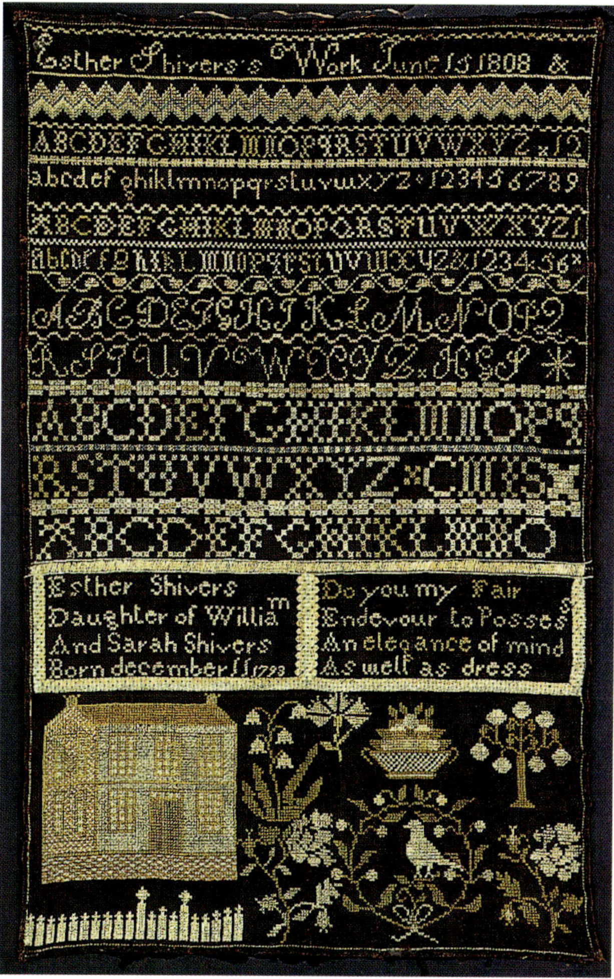

Figure 96. Sampler by Esther Shivers, age fourteen, dated June 15, 1808; attributed to south of the James River, Virginia. Esther was the daughter of William and Sarah Shivers of Nansemond County, Virginia. A detail of Esther's sampler is shown in figure 2.

Silk on linen ground of 25 x 26 threads per in. (ground is two pieces of linen seamed together); 16 3/4 in. x 26 in. Stitches: cross, eyelet, hem, herringbone, long arm cross, marking cross, queen's. *The Loudoun Museum; Bequest of Joan Stephens*

Figure 97. Sampler by Sarah Bruce Butt, age thirteen, dated June 18, 1811; attributed to south of the James River, Virginia. Sarah was the daughter of Nathaniel and Frances Butt of lower Norfolk County, Virginia. The reverse side of this sampler is illustrated on the back cover of this catalog.

Silk on linen ground of 27 x 35 threads per in.; 16 3/4 in. x 24 1/4 in. Stitches: cross, double cross, eyelet, four-sided, hem, marking cross, queen's.

1989-34

Figure 98. Sampler by Mary A. D. Craddock, age eleven, dated December 13, 1813; possibly south of the James River, Virginia. Where this sampler was worked and its exact relationship to the group are yet to be determined.

Silk on linen ground of 26 x 24 threads per in.; 16 1/4 in. x 21 1/2 in. Stitches: cross, double cross, eyelet, four-sided, herringbone, Irish, queen's, satin, tent.

1995-85

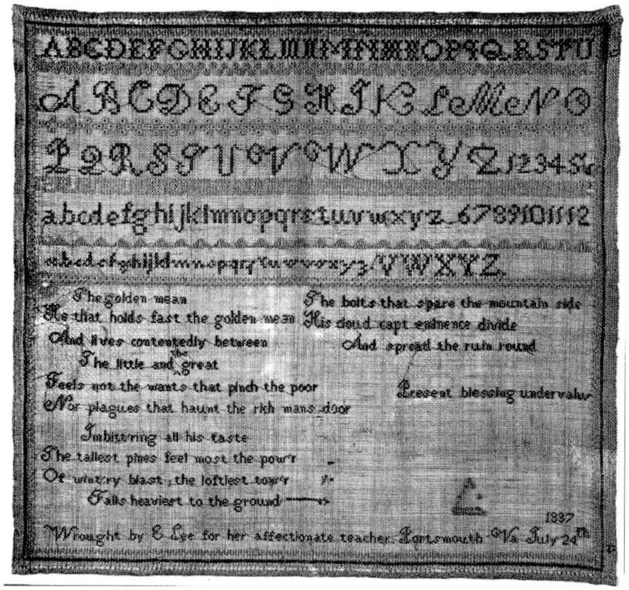

Figure 99. Sampler by E. Lee, dated July 24, 1837; "Portsmouth," Virginia.

Silk on linen ground of 25 x 24 threads per in. with stitches added later in wool; 18 in. x 16 1/2 in. Stitches: cross, double cross, eyelet, four-sided, hem, queen's, satin.

G1988-477; Purchased with funds from the Antique Collectors' Guild in memory of G. Conner McGehee, Jr.

Figure 100. Sampler by Eliza Kitching, age thirteen, dated 1829; "Bethlehem" Crossroads, Southampton County, Virginia.

Silk on linen ground of 25 x 21 threads per in.; 17 in. x 15 7/8 in. Stitches: cross, double cross, eyelet, Irish, outline, queen's, tent.

1991-149,A

Figure 100A. Detail of a building, possibly the Naval Hospital, from Eliza Kitching's sampler.

markedly realistic house with raised details on the porch and handrail. She may have been the daughter of John and Betsey Jackson DePriest Craddock, whose marriage bond of June 19, 1793, appeared in Henrico County, a district surrounding the city of Richmond. She also may have been the Mary Ann D. Craddock of Richmond who married Thomas T. Dickinson in 1821.[54]

The identity of the teacher—or teachers—who was responsible for the style of these four samplers is currently unknown. Nor is it clear whether she was a Quaker or had received training from a Quaker teacher.

An unfinished sampler depicting a Quaker-style alphabet gives the reader an insight into the influence of one schoolmistress and the close relationship she had with one of her students (fig. 99). On her sampler, Miss E. Lee worked a brief commemoration of the instructor who taught her in Portsmouth, Virginia: "Wrought by E. Lee for her affectionate teacher." Perhaps if Miss Lee had completed her sampler she might have stitched a house in the bottom right corner, as did Eliza Kitching (fig. 100). Although Eliza finished her sampler eight years earlier, the similarities between the two pieces suggest that they were stitched under the instruction of the same "affectionate teacher." Eliza's magnificent house may have been inspired by the Portsmouth Naval Hospital, construction of which began in 1829 (fig. 100A).[55] Her sampler is inscribed "Bethlehem," a reference to Bethlehem Crossroads in Southampton County (not to be confused with the Moravian town of Bethlehem, Pennsylvania).

Figure 101. Sampler by Elizabeth Eastham, dated July 11, 1831; "Wood Lawn School," Virginia. Little is known of the Eastham sisters. The initials on both of their samplers do not appear to be of family members but rather those of schoolmates or friends.

Silk on linen ground of 29 x 34 threads per in.; 16 1/4 in. x 24 1/2 in. Stitches: cross, eyelet, four-sided, star.
Esther C. White and Alma B. White

Figure 101A. Detail, "an emblem of innocence," from Elizabeth Eastham's sampler.

Wood Lawn School

Two samplers worked by sisters Martha and Elizabeth Eastham are clearly the products of Quaker influence (figs. 101 and 102). The sprigs of flowers, pairs of birds, geometric medallions, and the inscription "an emblem of innocence" are typical of Quaker work, suggesting that their teacher, Mrs. Saunders, had received Quaker instruction (fig. 101A). Both samplers are inscribed, "wrought at Wood Lawn School / in the year 1831 / Mrs. Frances G. Saunders Tutoress." The identification of "Wood Lawn School" is complicated by the fact that there were at least four different Virginia houses by this name during the period. One likely possibility is Woodlawn in King and Queen County. Sometime after 1824, the owner, Miranda Gaines, conducted a popular female seminary there.[56]

Designs and Patterns

Just as in the North, teachers, professional painters, and embroiderers provided most of the patterns for Virginian needlework pictures and samplers. They imported British and Continental prints, paintings, drawings, and needlework patterns for sale or rent. For example, Mrs. Tennant of Norfolk (the same instructor introduced in chapter three) advertised in 1796, "To enable her to teach from the most approved methods, as in Britian, she has procured at a very great expense a large and general assortment of stamps, of the most fashionable patterns."[57] These stamps produced repeating designs and configurations rather than complete compositions. Some teachers even provided their own original drawings at a lower cost; however, these originals were often simpler renditions of published drawings and prints.

An entry in the diary of Philip Fithian, tutor to the children of Robert Carter III of Nomini Hall in Westmoreland County, gives us an indication of how

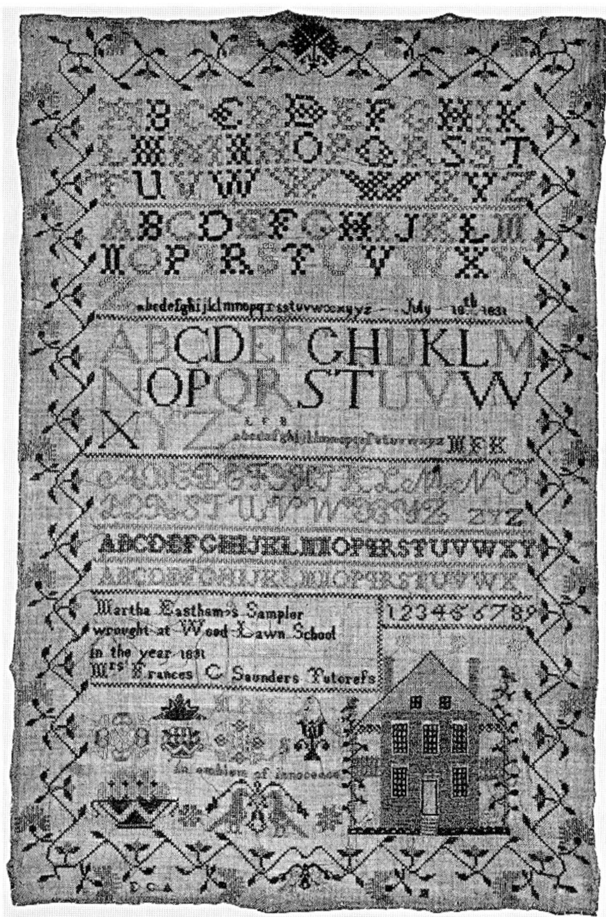

Figure 102. Sampler by Martha Eastham, dated July 11, 1831; "Wood Lawn School," Virginia.
Silk on linen ground of 29 x 29 threads per in.; 17 1/2 in. x 25 1/2 in. Stitches: cross, eyelet, four-sided, outline, star.
Esther C. White and Alma B. White

Figure 103. Unfinished petticoat border, 1750–1775; attributed to Gates County, North Carolina. Family history states that this petticoat border was owned by a member of the Bethea family of Chowan Precinct, North Carolina. It was hand-drawn in ink to be embroidered but never started.

Linen and cotton with inked design; 82 1/2 in. x 5 1/2 in.
G1979-1; Gift of Mrs. Bettyanne B. Twigg

designs might have been created for the needleworker, although in this instance the design was not intended for a sampler. He wrote in his diary in 1773, in the "evening, at Miss Prissy's request I drew for her some flowers on linen which she is going to imbroider, for a various counterpane."[58] Perhaps his drawing looked similar to an unfinished petticoat border attributed to the Bethea family of North Carolina (fig. 103). The design was drawn by hand in ink on a linen and cotton ground but never embroidered.

One advertisement in 1784 actually offered young ladies instruction in pattern drawing:

> MR. MORRIS, EMBROIDERER, TAMBOUR WORKER, and PATTERN DRAWER, lately arrived from LONDON, is desirous to instruct YOUNG LADIES in the above-mentioned polite and fashionable arts, and which he flatters himself can be effected in a short time, so that a lady may become perfectly mistress of these essentially necessary branches of education.[59]

The original inked outline of the design can still be seen in some areas of a memorial sampler worked by Margaret J. Cross in 1829 (figs. 104 and 104A).

"Palemon and Levinia"

Virginia echoed the educational goals of the rest of America in the late eighteenth and early nineteenth centuries. For girls this meant the proficient duplication in embroidery of idealized themes that were widely recognized and approved of, rather than the development of individual creativity. These subjects were often inspired by stories from the Bible and classical writings. Needlework compositions were taken from existing illustrations, usually English or Continental engravings or other printed images.

During the first two decades of the nineteenth century the parable of Palemon and Lavinia—a romanticized version of the Biblical tale of Ruth and Boaz—was a popular theme, appearing on embroideries worked in Massachusetts, Pennsylvania, and Virginia.[60] As told by James Thomson (1700–1748) in the "Autumn" passage of his extraordinarily popular poem *The Seasons* (published in Philadelphia in 1804), the updated narrative repeats the Old Testament themes of unselfish devotion and human kindness over and above conventional duty and the importance of family status.[61] Left impoverished

Figure 104. Sampler by Margaret J. Cross, age twelve, dated April 30, 1829; attributed to Suffolk, Virginia, or Gates County, North Carolina. Margaret Jane Cross completed her sampler in memory of her father, Taylor Cross, four years after his death in 1825.

Silk and crinkled silk on linen ground of 34 x 29 threads per in.; 21 in. x 17 3/4 in. Stitches: chain, cross, outline, satin, straight.
1996-804

Figure 104A. Detail of Margaret Cross's sampler, showing black ink outlines around the leaves.

after her father's death, Lavinia, a humble gleaner, works in the fields of the wealthy young landowner Palemon. The story unfolds to reveal that Lavinia is the long-sought-for daughter of Palemon's old patron and friend, Acasto. Discovering this, Palemon is finally able to court and marry Lavinia, preserving the social order and at the same time rewarding Lavinia for her exceptional goodness and devotion. Although this parable is less familiar to us today, its messages concerning social status and female humility would have been recognized by the makers of these embroideries.

Composed of costly materials such as embroidery threads, ground, and ribbon, all of silk, with mica and metal sequins, Mary Abney's and Drusilla De La Fayette Tate's pictures of Palemon and Lavinia

Figure 105. Needlework picture by Mary Abney, ca. 1802; attributed to Virginia, possibly Rockbridge County.

Silk and chenille on silk and a linen ground of 62 x 62 threads per in. with silk ribbon, mica, metal sequins, padding, and watercolor; 15 3/4 in. x 17 in. Stitches: bullion knot, cross, French knot, outline, satin, split.
1989-304,A

Figure 105A. Detail of pastoral scene in Mary Abney's sampler.

proclaimed their families' ability to pay for advanced needlework instruction (figs. 105, 105A, 106). In the 1810 Virginia census Abney is a surname that appears in Rockbridge County, Virginia. Drusilla De La Fayette Tate may have grown up in or near Rockbridge County, where she subsequently married Dr. John D. Ewing and lived as an adult.[62] These two girls undoubtedly worked their thematically sophisticated and beautifully executed pictures under the careful guidance of a skilled needlework teacher who had access to the most fashionable print

Figure 106. Needlework picture by Drusilla De La Fayette Tate, dated 1802; attributed to Virginia, possibly Rockbridge County.
Silk on silk and linen ground of 48 x 50 threads per in. with silk ribbon, mica, padding, and watercolor; 17 1/2 in. x 17 3/8 in.
Stitches: bullion knot, buttonhole, cross, French knot, satin, tent.
Private collection; Photograph courtesy the Museum of Early Southern Decorative Arts

Figure 107. Detail of whitework bedcover by Sarah (Salley) B. Wisdom (Mrs. Alexander Fulcher), dated 1818; attributed to Richmond, Virginia. This bedcover descended in the maker's family until 1981, when it was acquired by the Abby Aldrich Rockefeller Folk Art Center.
White cotton on a white cotton ground; 87 1/2 in. x 106 in.
Stitches: buttonhole, chain variation, coral knot, feather, flat, outline, satin, seed, stem.
AARFAC, 81.609.3

sources and materials of the day. Yet to be identified is the teacher or school responsible for these superb embroideries. Whether the girls attended a local seminary or were sent away for an education is yet to be determined.

Sarah B. Wisdom's embroidered bedcover was inspired by an engraving of Palemon and Lavinia published in Thomson's book *The Seasons, with the Castle of Indolence Poems* (fig. 107).[63] Sarah used a wide variety of ornamental stitches to create different textures in the embroidered designs. Born in Virginia in 1796, Sarah B. Wisdom was the daughter of Tavnor W. Wisdom, a well-to-do planter of

Figure 108. Needlework picture by Sarah S. Dana, ca. 1805; attributed to Dorchester, Massachusetts. Sarah was a proficient needleworker. A second silk and watercolor picture she worked as a memorial to deceased family members is also in the Abby Aldrich Rockefeller Folk Art Center collection.

Silk on silk ground with watercolor and ink; in original frame with gold on black eglomisé (reverse painting on glass) mat measuring 11 1/2 in. x 17 1/2 in. Stitches: cross, four-sided, outline, satin, straight.
AARFAC, 79.601.2

Spotsylvania County, Virginia. She is said to have begun work on this spectacular piece in 1812 and to have finished it in 1818, the year inscribed on the cover. The embroidered names "Alexander & Salley B. Fulcher" commemorate her marriage on January 2, 1812, to Alexander Fulcher of Richmond and Goochland Counties. Together they had seven children. In 1831 Alexander and Salley Fulcher moved to Kentucky, where they resided until their respective deaths in 1853 and 1873.[64]

Compare these Virginia examples with Sarah Sumner Dana's splendid embroidery of Palemon and Lavinea, worked presumably while she was a student at Mrs. Saunders's and Miss Beach's Academy in Dorchester, Massachusetts (fig. 108).[65] Her picture portrays the moment described in Thomson's "Autumn" when Palemon recognizes that Lavinia is the daughter of Acasto. Embroidered at the bottom of the picture is a line from the poem, "O heaven! The very same / The soften'd image of my noble friend! / Thomson." The composition is probably based on a print source different from that of the other embroideries shown here.

Nineteenth-Century Virginia Sampler Makers and Their Teachers

Samplers and needlework pictures were worked in almost every city and county of Virginia from 1742 to the mid-nineteenth century. Created by girls from age six to young womanhood, they demonstrate a variety of materials, stitches, designs, and levels of skill. At present eighteen groups of samplers, two from the eighteenth century and sixteen from the nineteenth, have been identified, each with distinguishing characteristics that reflect the influence of one teacher or school.[66]

Most Virginia samplers were worked in silk embroidery threads on a natural color linen fabric. As we have seen, these were the typical materials used in America from the seventeenth century to well into the nineteenth. The silk and linen were imported from Europe through England and sold at local Virginia stores. Very few Virginia samplers were made on locally woven grounds. For example, in 1772 Mrs. Rathell, a Williamsburg shopkeeper, wrote to her agent in England requesting needlework supplies: "I am in Much distress for them, the undernaith Articles without fail—3 Dozn bunches of Pink Shenell [chenille embroidery thread] & 3 Dozn D[itt]o of blue Sheneele & No Other Coulars."[67]

Richmond

The move of the capital of Virginia from Williamsburg to Richmond in 1780 coincided with a period of growth in female education. From 1780 to 1840 numerous private seminaries and academies for girls were established throughout Virginia, especially in the larger cities of Norfolk, Fredericksburg, and Richmond. Exactly what the components of female education should be was widely debated. Some advocated polite and ornamental accomplishments such as fancy embroidery, drawing, music, and French. Others recommended academic education more closely paralleling that of boys. Rosalie Stier Calvert complained in 1804, "The education of young girls here [in America] is quite mistaken at present. They bring them up as if they are going to marry dukes and marquises, and then [the girls] don't ensnare anybody because the men are afraid of their airs and expenses."[68] One 1786 school advertisement in the *Virginia Independent Chronicle* is of special interest because it compares the education of girls and boys at that time:

> The girls on Saturdays will be taught plain Needle Work, and the Duties incumbent on Mistresses of Families. No other Difference will be made between the Education of Boys and Girls, except that the Girls will not be taught Mathematics.[69]

Richmond newspaper advertisements boasted of teachers ready to receive girls whose parents could afford the tuition as well as would show an interest in educating their daughters. Most teachers provided fundamental instruction in reading, writing,

Figure 109. Sampler by Elizabeth Ellett, probably 1815–1820; probably Richmond, Virginia.
Silk on linen ground of 28 x 32 threads per in.; 17 in. x 21 1/2 in. Stitches: cross, double cross, eyelet, queen's.
Valentine Museum, 39.23.8

Figure 110. Sampler by Nancy Prentis Barber, age nine or ten, dated 1800; "Richmond," Virginia.

Silk on linen ground of 56 x 64 threads per in.; 21 1/4 in. x 19 in. Stitches: chain, cross variation, double cross, herringbone, outline, satin.

1987-34, A-B

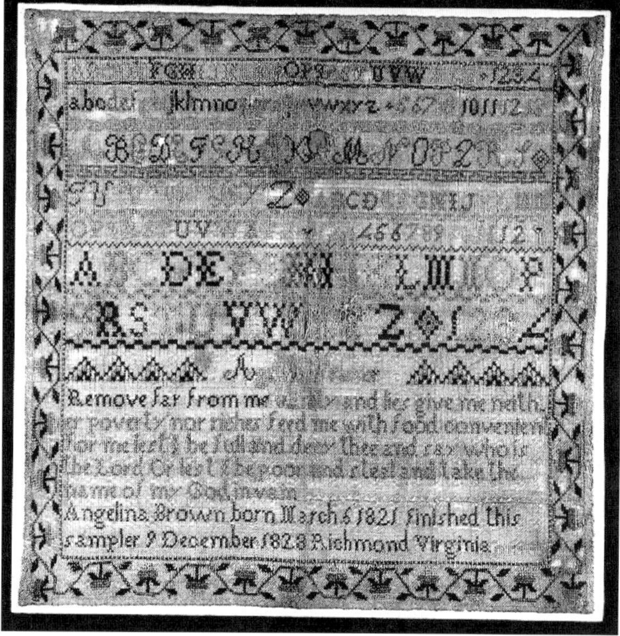

Figure 111. Sampler by Angelina Brown, age seven, dated December 9, 1828; "Richmond," Virginia. This was probably the first of at least two samplers that we know Angelina Brown stitched between 1828 and 1829. The name Agur in "Agur's Prayer" is that of an unknown sage who compiled Proverbs 30.

Silk on linen ground of 28 x 32 threads per in.; 16 1/2 in. x 17 in. Stitches: cross, double cross, eyelet, four-sided, satin.

Valentine Museum, 1898.29.3

ciphering, and plain work. In addition to these basics, many offered advanced lessons in a variety of fancy work, including silk embroideries in chenille and metallic threads, filigree, tambour, and openwork. Almost all teachers noted the care and watchful attention that would be given to the manners and moral deportment of their pupils.

Elizabeth Ellett's beautiful sampler (fig. 109) is very similar to one not shown here that was worked by Mary L. Clements in 1817. The stylized carnation with flanking floral sprays and birds is seen on both pieces. Initial research places the two girls in the Richmond region. One sampler that certainly was made in Richmond is Nancy Prentis Barber's work, marked "Finisheb this Anna Dommina 1800 / Richmonb Virginia" (fig. 110). The extremely fine ground fabric and lacy effect of the realistically worked undulating floral and vine border are characteristics seen in other embroideries stitched in Richmond. The school or teacher responsible for

Figure 112. Sampler by Angelina Brown, age eight, dated August 27, 1829; Richmond, Virginia.
Silk on linen ground of 31 x 30 threads per in.; 14 1/4 in. x 16 5/8 in. Stitches: chain, cross, double cross, eyelet, four-sided, herringbone, Irish, satin.
Valentine Museum, 1898.29.2

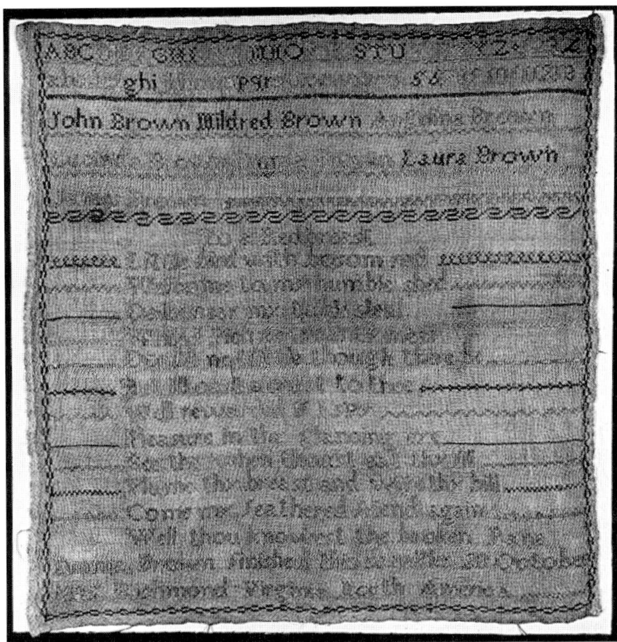

Figure 113. Sampler by Emma Brown, dated October 28, 1835; "Richmond," Virginia. In addition to the poem "To a Redbreast," Emma Brown stitched her parents' and siblings' names.
Silk on linen ground of 28 x 28 threads per in.; 15 7/8 in. x 16 3/8 in. Stitches: back, cross, double cross.
Valentine Museum, 1898.29.1

these delicate works is yet to be identified. Nancy's sampler provides an unusual glimpse into her life. She included what are probably her parents' names, Janet and Paul, and other family initials on the sampler. But it is curious that she reversed most of the instances of the letters a, b, d, t, and n. Perhaps Nancy had a learning disorder such as dyslexia.[70]

Angelina Brown stitched two samplers, in 1828 and 1829. Eight months after completing her first sampler, at the age of just seven, Angelina finished a second (figs. 111 and 112). In that interim she had added three additional stitches to her needlework vocabulary. In 1835 a younger family member, Emma, worked a sampler (fig. 113) which included a poem, "To a Redbreast." All three samplers were found in the Wickham-Valentine House of Richmond in 1898 and were the first to be accessioned by the then newly formed Valentine Museum.[71] The relationship among the Brown, Valentine, and Wickham families is yet to be determined.

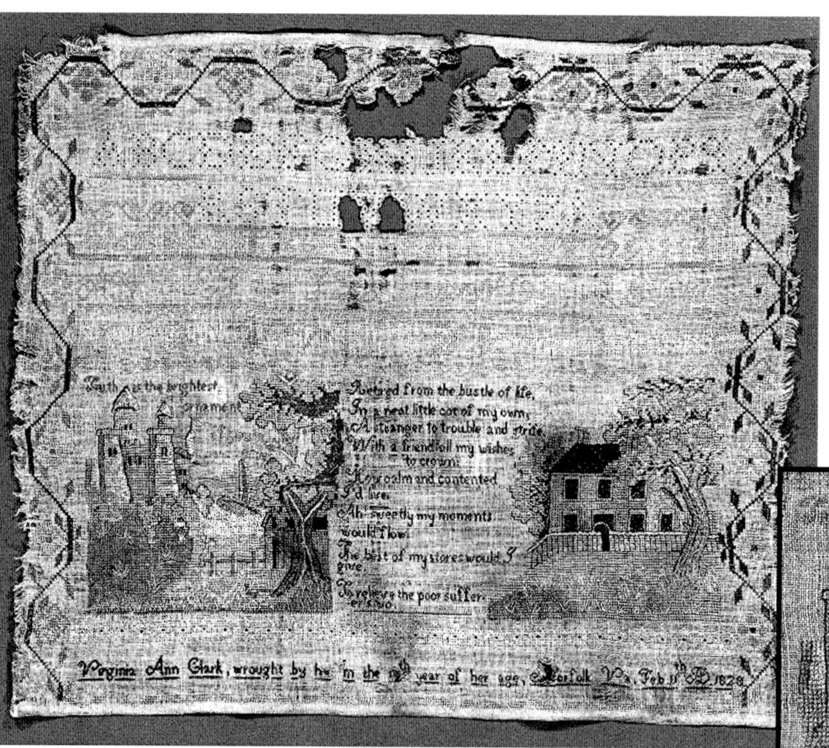

Figure 114. Sampler by Virginia Ann Clark, age "1[?]," dated February 11, 1828; "Norfolk, Va."
Silk on linen ground of 30 x 31 threads per in.; 17 1/8 in. x 20 1/2 in. Stitches: back, chain, cross, cross variations, four-sided, eyelet, long arm cross, marking cross, satin, straight.
1986-10

Figure 114A. Detail of Virginia Ann Clark's sampler.

Norfolk

Two Norfolk samplers were worked under the direction of the same anonymous needlework teacher in the second decade of the nineteenth century (figs. 114 and 115). There was no lack of teachers or seminaries in the city during this time. For example, two rival schools, the "Young Ladies Seminary, MAIN-STREET" and "FEMALE SEMINARY, GRANBY-STREET" advertised within months of each other in 1820. Some of the "polite branches of Education" offered by Mrs. Barron and Mrs. Russell of the "Young Ladies Seminary" were "Worsted and Rug work, embroidery, and Fancy Work of every description; Sampler Work and Plain Sewing."[72] The densely worked scenes in the bottom sections of these Norfolk samplers were probably based on prints of the period (fig. 114A).

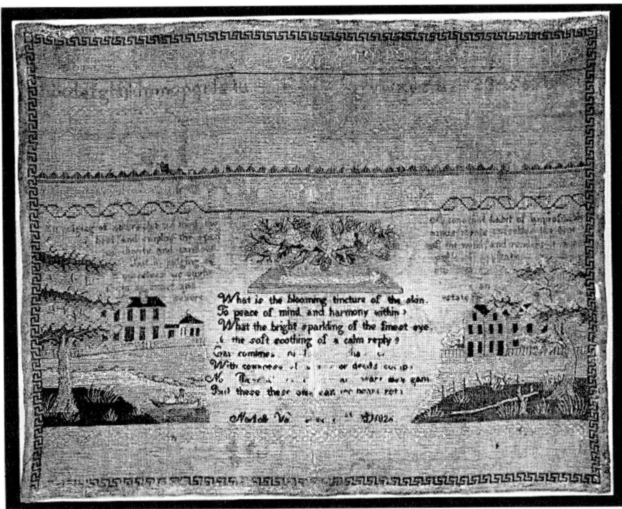

Figure 115. Sampler by unknown maker, dated 1826; "Norfolk, Va."
Silk on linen ground of 29 x 33 threads per in.; 21 1/2 in. x 17 in. Stitches: back, cross, double cross, flat, four-sided, herringbone, outline, queen's, satin, straight.
1996-825

Loudoun County

A number of embroideries made in Loudoun County, Virginia, during the nineteenth century has survived.[73] One of the most charming is Martha Dandridge Ball's needlework picture, probably made between 1815 and 1820 (fig. 116). It is worked in silk embroidery threads and watercolor on the unusual ground fabric of worsted, sometimes referred to as tammy (fig. 116A). Another Loudoun County girl, Lucinda Ish, stitched two samplers between the months of February and May in 1812. After completing her first sampler of alphabets and numbers, Lucinda worked a fairly elaborate embroidery featuring a grand two-storied brick house and oversized birds (figs. 117 and 118).

Lynchburg

Mary Kennerly may have attended one of the several schools for female education that were advertised in local Lynchburg newspapers during the second decade of the nineteenth century (fig. 119). For example, in 1814 John and Sarah Pryor advertised in the *Lynchburg Press* the opening of their Lynchburg Female Academy, "instructing females in the various branches of ornamental & scientific education; viz. Needle work in its various branches, Embroidery and drawing, painting and Pin work; Spelling, reading, writing and Arithmetic."[74] Two samplers, not illustrated here, are related to Mary's work. Susanah S. Rees of Lynchburg depicted a more primitive view of the buildings seen on Mary's sampler.[75] Both Susanah Rees and Catherine Louisa Steele, from Tennessee, stitched similar diamond-shaped and Irish stitch designs, an alphabet worked in four-sided stitches, and a double birdcage.[76] Some of the Kennerly family moved westward, as did other families from Lynchburg.[77] Is it possible that they carried this sampler style with them?

Shenandoah and Rockingham Counties: "Yellow House" Samplers

A collection of samplers worked in Shenandoah and Rockingham Counties is distinguished by a prominently centered yellow house, fence, bold vine border, and sawtooth band.[78] This group, stitched between 1824 and 1845, illustrates the continuation of a traditional needlework style into a period when such embroidery was being replaced by Berlin work. During this period the town of New Market was a Lutheran stronghold and center of influence. Was the persistence of this sampler style due to the conservative German and Lutheran population of these counties, or were other forces at work?

Figure 116. Needlework picture by Martha D[andridge] Ball, ca. 1815; attributed to Loudoun County, Virginia. Martha Dandridge Ball, grandniece of George Washington, was born on October 6, 1799, probably at her parents' home, Springwood, in Loudoun County. She was the daughter of Colonel Burgess Ball and Frances Washington. It is not known where Martha lived after the death of her father in 1800. She married Colonel Catlett Gibson and had two daughters before she died in 1823 (Horace Edwin Hayden, *Virginia Genealogies: A Genealogy of the Glassell Family of Scotland and Virginia*, pp. 111–117).

Silk and watercolor on wool ground of 59 x 53 threads per in.; 14 7/8 in. x 12 1/2 in. Stitches: chain, outline, satin, straight.

G1991-595; Purchased with gift funds from Mrs. Joan Rozier Stephens

Figure 116A. Detail of Martha Ball's sampler.

Figure 117. Sampler by Lucinda Ish, age twelve, dated February 26, 1812; "Loudoun County, Virginia." Lucinda Ish was born on December 22, 1799, to Jacob and Susannah King Ish of Loudoun County, where Jacob was a successful tanner and member of the Reformed Church. In 1817 she married John Rouse Adams. The Adamses' young family moved west in search of land and opportunity, settling in Shelby County, Tennessee, around 1830. Lucinda died there in 1839 or 1840 (MESDA, accession file 2033-6, and notes from owner).

Silk and cotton on linen ground of 24 x 25 threads per in.; 15 in. x 20 3/4 in. Stitches: cross, double cross, eyelet, four-sided, hem, herringbone, marking cross, queen's.
Elizabeth Adams Lane, Lucinda's great-great-granddaughter

Figure 118. Sampler by Lucinda Ish, age twelve, dated May 12, 1812; "Loudoun County, Virginia."

Silk on linen ground; 20 3/4 in. x 25 in. Stitches: cross, herringbone, Irish, queen's, satin, and stem.
Photograph courtesy Museum of Early Southern Decorative Arts

Figure 119. Sampler by Mary Kennerly, age seven, dated 1815; "Lynchburg," Virginia.
Silk on linen ground of 27 x 27 threads per in.; 16 1/8 in. x 24 3/4 in. Stitches: back, cross, eyelet, flat, four-sided, hem, Irish, queen's, satin, tent.
1987-687

Figure 120. Sampler by Levinea Campbell, age fourteen, dated 1824; attributed to Rockingham County, Virginia.
Silk on linen ground of 34 x 38 threads per in.; 16 3/4 in. x 17 3/4 in. Stitches: cross, eyelet, flat, satin.
Charles and Elizabeth Umstott

The earliest known sampler in this group is the work of Levinia Campbell, finished in 1824 (fig. 120). She included the characteristic New Market sawtooth band and a yellow house with fence. Her work, however, is more closely related to an 1845 sampler, not illustrated here, inscribed "Rockingham Country Virginia."[79]

Mahala Cline's sampler, dated 1830 and inscribed "New Market," appears to be a transitional piece with characteristics of both the earlier sampler by Lavinea Campbell and later New Market samplers (fig. 121). Mahala was probably a member of the Shenandoah County Cline family, which was closely associated with the Lutheran churches in the area. Between 1825 and 1866 the Reverend J. P. Cline

Figure 121. Sampler by Mahala Cline, dated April 19, 1830; "New Market," Shenandoah County, Virginia.
Silk on linen ground of 29 x 29 threads per in.; 18 1/2 in. x 18 in. Stitches: cross, eyelet, herringbone, queen's, satin.
1994-1; Purchased partially with funds donated by Mrs. Harold A. Via, Jr., in memory of Mrs. W. Peyton May

Figure 122. Sampler by Eleanora C. Hankel, dated April 18, 1838; "New Market," Shenandoah County, Virginia.
Silk on linen ground.
Private collection

served intermittently as the pastor for St. Matthew Evangelical Lutheran Church in New Market. The church had been founded in 1790 by the Reverend Paul Henkel. In 1825 Henry Cline, along with other trustees, advertised in the *Shenandoah Herald* for a teacher at Zion's Church, built jointly by the Lutherans and the German Reformed.[80] Perhaps it was here that Mahala stitched her sampler.

Eleanora Hankel's sampler is one of at least three New Market samplers worked in the 1840s (fig. 122).[81] Eleanora was a member of the prominent Henkel family of Shenandoah County. The Henkels were well-known theologians, printers, and patrons of learning in Shenandoah and neighboring counties. The yellow house depicted on these samplers may represent the locally acclaimed Henkel home and printing shop. Established in 1806 by Ambrose Henkel, the printing press was operated by the family for more than one hundred years.[82] In 1850 Samuel G. Henkel was one of the twelve trustees of the New Market Female Seminary. In 1854, S. Henkel was principal of the Female Seminary at New Market.[83] It is probable that these later "yellow house" samplers were worked at the Female Seminary.

Figure 123. Sampler by Unity A. Delk, dated September 5, 1834; attributed to Isle of Wight County, Virginia.

Silk on linen ground of 27 x 30 threads per in. with paper lining; original frame and glass; 17 1/4 in. x 20 1/2 in. Stitches: chain, cross, four-sided, outline.

Ms. Martha Wren Briggs

Figure 124. Sampler by Elizabeth M. Cofer, age sixteen, dated 1834; attributed to Isle of Wight County, Virginia.

Silk on linen ground of 28 x 29 threads per in. with paper lining; original frame and glass, 17 1/2 in. x 20 7/8 in. Stitches: chain, cross, double cross, eyelet, four-sided, outline, straight.

G1988-461; Gift from the estate of Mary Wren Cofer Ballard in honor of her daughters, Mary Wren Ballard Oliver and Anne Lewis Ballard Weaver

Southampton, Surry, and Isle of Wight Counties

Unity A. Delk and Elizabeth M. Cofer worked almost identical samplers to honor the deaths of their respective parents, Wiley Jones Delk and Jerusha Lancaster Cofer (figs. 123 and 124). Not shown here is an earlier sampler worked by Unity's older sister, Martha, which also commemorates the death of their father. In 1824, four years after the death of Wiley Delk, his widow, Martha Wren Delk, of Southampton County, married Joseph Cofer, a Baptist minister from Isle of Wight and Surry Counties. One year earlier Joseph's first wife,

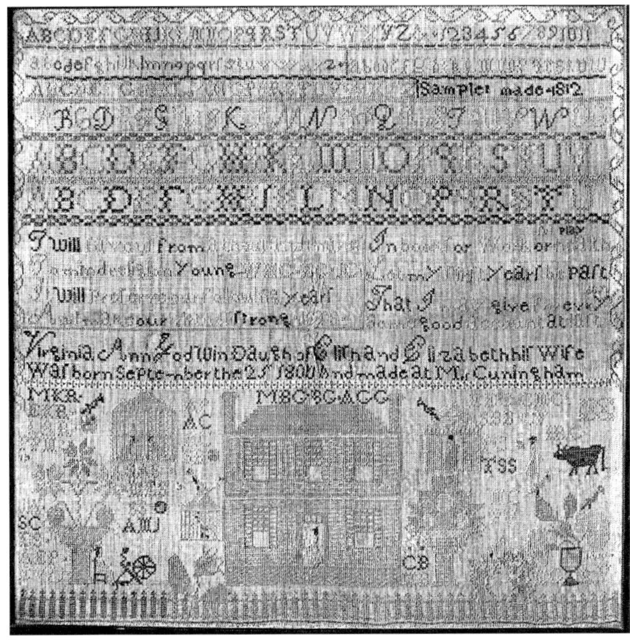

Figure 125. Sampler by Virginia Ann Godwin, ca. 1816; Isle of Wight County, Virginia.
Probably silk on linen.
Private collection; Photograph courtesy Museum of Early Southern Decorative Arts

Figure 126. Drawing inscribed "Drawn for Miss Caroline E. Vellines," 1835–1840, by Jason M. Delk. Watercolor and ink; Southampton or Isle of Wight County, Virginia.
19 in. x 13 3/4 in.
Mrs. Adeline B. Ransone

Jerusha Cofer, had died, leaving him with ten children ranging in ages from twenty-three to five, the youngest being the aforementioned Elizabeth. When Martha Wren Delk married Joseph Cofer, she became Elizabeth's stepmother; Martha and Unity Delk became Elizabeth's stepsisters.[84]

The three girls worked their samplers under the direction of the same needlework teacher. One likely candidate is Mrs. Rachel Cunningham, who operated a seminary on Red Point, "opposite to Smithfield, Isle of Wight." In 1816 she advertised her continuing instruction in "Spelling, Reading, Writing, Drawing, Painting, and Needle-Work."[85] An earlier sampler worked by Virginia Godwin and inscribed "made at Mrs. Cuningham" features a similar house with open windows, fence, and placement of family initials (fig. 125).

The three-and-one-half-storied house labeled "Arcade No. 3" on Elizabeth Cofer's sampler has not been located. However, many of the sets of initials appearing on the sampler have been identified as Elizabeth's siblings and other family members. The most prominent initials, J. C. and M. C., which flank the chimneys, represent her father, Joseph Cofer, and her stepmother, Martha Delk Cofer. Like Elizabeth, Unity A. Delk stitched the initials J. C. and M. C. for her stepfather and mother as well as other family initials. Yet to be determined is the significance of

"Mount Pleasant," which appears above Unity's two-storied house.

Interestingly, a related watercolor drawing entitled "Drawn for Miss Caroline Vellines," by another family member, Jason M. Delk, features a house not dissimilar to the house on Elizabeth's and Unity's samplers (fig. 126). Caroline later worked a sampler, not illustrated here, depicting this exact building. She eventually married Martha Delk's twin brother.

The "Open Windows" Samplers

Made between the years 1817 and 1848, a group of five samplers with remarkable similarities presents the researcher with a series of questions. The most noticeable characteristics of these embroideries are family names and houses with open windows, whose styles vary only slightly. Other shared elements are vine and bud borders, identical alphabets, and stanzas from a verse entitled "On Religion." The families of the girls appear to be related by marriage as well as belong to the same social and economic class.

Most problematic are the place-names that appear on the samplers: "Greenwood Seminary," "Eastern View," "Mount Airy," "Poplar Grove," "Cedar Hill," and "Rose Vale." Popular names during this period, they appear in at least two neighboring counties and as many as six, the most notable being Hanover, Orange, Caroline, and Spotsylvania. Four samplers are inscribed with two place-names each, perhaps identifying both the homes of the stitchers and the schools where the pieces were worked. Only two include the same name, Eastern View. Were these locations the girls' dwellings, the teachers' schools, family estates, or other local prominent residences? The answers to these questions are not completely clear.

Mary W. Tomlin's sampler, inscribed "Greenwood Seminary," is the earliest of this fascinating group of samplers (fig. 127). The identification of Greenwood Seminary has been problematic. No documentation has been found for the school, and at least five different Greenwoods have been located in the neighboring counties of Hanover, Caroline, Orange, Spotsylvania, and Culpeper. Mary Williamson Tomlin was one of six children born to John Walker and Margaret Williamson Ball Tomlin of Clifton in Hanover County, Virginia. She married Dr. Corbin Braxton, and together they had at least five children.[86]

Martha Smith stitched the names of her parents, Caleb Smith and Mary W. Smith, of King George County, Virginia, and the name Eliza, probably for a sister, at the top of her sampler (fig. 128). The name Ann Norris stitched in the left bottom corner may identify Martha's needlework teacher. The similarities between Martha's and Mary Tomlin's samplers are striking, especially in the houses and flanking trees. Also notable are the appearance of the parents' names at the top of each sampler, the identical alphabets, and outer borders of vines and buds. Clearly these two samplers were worked under the same instructor. Yet to be determined is the needlework teacher responsible for this unique style.

An important feature of the latest three samplers in this group is the inclusion of the teacher's name, Miss Lucy Mary Quisenberry, also listed as Mrs. Lucy M. Montague. Miss Quisenberry does not appear to have been the originator of the open windows group; more likely she was one of the designer's earliest students. Providing instruction in needlework from at least 1835 to 1848, Mrs. Lucy Mary Quisenberry Montague perpetuated a style that illustrates the enduring nature of traditional sampler making.

Mildred B. Chewning marked her sampler with her name and the following piece of information: "commenced and completed this sampler with Miss Lucy Mary Quisenberry at Mount Airy in the year

1835" (fig. 129). Mount Airy may refer to the home of Humphrey Hill in Caroline County. In 1802 Hill insured the schoolhouse on his property for $150.00.[87] In an 1811 advertisement in the *Virginia Argus*, Hill informed the public that "FEMALE EDUCATION, will be continued at Mountairy—under the direction of Miss TERREL."[88] Mildred B. Chewning was a member of the large Chewning family of Louisa and Spotsylvania Counties. Miss Lucy Quisenberry's half brother, Elijah Quisenberry, lived at Rose Valley, Spotsylvania County, possibly the same location Mildred named on her sampler as Rose Vale.[89]

Martha J. Cosby also marked her sampler with her name and "commenced and completed this sampler with Mrs. Lucy M. Montague in the year 1844 Eastern View" (figs. 130 and 130A). Sometime between 1835 and 1844 Miss Quisenberry married

Figure 128. Sampler by Martha Smith, dated 1824; possibly Greenwood Seminary, Virginia.
Silk on linen ground; 16 1/4 in. x 16 1/2 in. Stitches: cross, double cross, flat.
Photograph courtesy the Daughters of the American Revolution Museum

Figure 127. Sampler by Mary W. Tomlin, age ten, "Greenwood Seminary," Virginia. Mary was born in 1807 and worked her sampler in 1817.
Silk on linen ground of 30 x 34 threads per in.; 17 3/4 in. x 17 1/2 in. Stitches: cross, double cross, flat, four-sided, herringbone variation, queen's.
1990-39

Figure 129. Sampler by Mildred B. Chewning, dated 1835; "Mount Airy," Virginia.

Silk on linen ground of 26 x 30 threads per in.; 19 3/4 in. x 20 1/4 in. Stitches: chain, cross, double cross, eyelet, four-sided, outline, satin. *Valentine Museum, 86.122*

Figure 130. Sampler by Martha J. Cosby, dated 1844; attributed to "Eastern View," Virginia.

Silk on linen ground of 31 x 30 threads per in.; 18 3/4 in. x 20 in. Stitches: bullion knot, buttonhole, cross, double cross, eyelet, flat, outline, satin.

Mrs. Ann Biscoe Johnson Behm

Figure 130A. Detail of Martha Cosby's sampler, showing dog tethered to a tree with a chain stitch lead.

Mr. Montague.[90] In contrast to many teachers who discontinued their vocations once they were married, Mrs. Montague continued to offer instructions in needlework until at least 1848. "Eastern View" has been located in both Caroline and Hanover Counties. "Poplar Grove," which is stitched on the sampler in the middle of the right side, has been located in Caroline County.

A fifth sampler was worked by Sarah E. Reynolds and marked, "Commenced and completed this sampler with her aunt Lucy M. Montague at Eastern View in the year 1848" (fig. 131). As is characteristic of these sampler makers, Sarah stitched a large number of family names on her sampler. The Reynolds and Quisenberry families were related several times by marriage.

A Final Note

One of the most perplexing aspects of researching Virginia samplers is that the place-names on these embroideries do not necessarily reflect their origins. This dilemma has been most clearly spelled out in the discussions of the last two sampler groups—the Southampton, Surry, and Isle of Wight Counties group and the "open windows" collection—in which similar or identical embroidered house motifs have been given different names by their young workers. Thus, the houses on these pieces may not be accurate representations of the place-names associated with them. The following eighteenth-century anecdote sheds light on one possible scenario. Olney Winsor, a Rhode Island merchant working in Alexandria in 1787, wrote home to his wife in February of that year concerning his search for a fitting building to be included on his daughter's sampler. At the time his daughter was attending Polly Balch's school in Providence. He concluded, "I could not send a Draft of a suitable building to put in Nancy's Sampler for we had none here. . . ."[91] Had Mr. Winsor found an appropriate Alexandria building for Nancy's sampler, the result would have puzzled modern scholars attempting to explain the presence of an Alexandria building on a sampler associated with other embroideries displaying the Providence State House! ❧

Figure 131 (opposite). Sampler by Sarah (Sallie) E. Reynolds, age twelve or thirteen, dated 1848; "Eastern View," Virginia.
Silk on linen ground of 34 x 30 threads per in.; 17 3/8 in. x 16 3/4 in. Stitches: chain, cross, double cross, eyelet, four-sided, outline.
Ellen Taylor Donnelly

Sarah Quisenberry
Let deep repentance, faith, and love,
Be join'd with godly fear;
all my conversation prove
heart to be sincere.
James S Reynolds
Let lively hope my soul inspire;
Let warm affections rise;
And may I wait with strong desire,
To mount above the skies!
William B Reynolds
Washington Reynolds
Sarah Coleman
Ann Reynolds
Mary Ann Reynolds
Benjamin Quisenbe
Lucy Jane Reynolds
Joseph D Reynolds
Eliza Catherine Reynolds
Lucie A Reynolds

EPILOGUE

I LEAVE THE READER with three observations. First, samplers are often enigmas that create more questions than are answered by the information so painstakingly stitched on them. It is these very questions, however, that can lead us to a better understanding of the sampler maker's world. How far did the young needleworker travel from family and friends to attend school, was she homesick or afraid, and did her parents feel it was their duty to send her to school—these queries help us understand changing attitudes toward female education in the latter part of the eighteenth century. Did the makers realize the significance of the verses and biblical stories they so carefully wrought on their samplers, and if so, what does this tell us about the moral upbringing of young women during the time period discussed? Questioning the extent to which the community at large influenced the design of samplers and the circumstances under which sampler styles were transferred provide the modern viewer with an insight into the larger forces at work in the making of a sampler: namely, religion, fashion trends, consumerism, and westward expansion.

Second, understanding the technology of sampler making—in this instance how the stitches were worked—is a valid method of identifying regional groups of samplers. Through the close examination of the backs of Virginia embroideries, the prevalent use of marking cross on colonial, eighteenth-, and some early nineteenth-century Virginia samplers has been firmly documented. This knowledge has assisted with establishing regional preferences and styles in Virginia work.

The third observation, and perhaps the one with the most far reaching implications, is that the role of the sampler in female education continuously changed, as did the definition of a female education, during the 180 years spanned in this catalog. In the seventeenth century female education consisted of whatever the teacher could teach for whoever could afford it. Early samplers worked as part of a schoolgirl's education might have been considered female rites of passage as well as stitching exercises. The haphazard approach to female education continued throughout much of the following century, yet samplers increasingly became indicators of social status. By the last decades of the eighteenth century the components of female education ranged from polite and ornamental accomplishments, such as fancy embroidery, drawing, music, and French, to an academic education more closely paralleling that of boys. In addition to teaching practical stitches samplers reinforced moral and religious lessons, which were often stitched on them by the needleworker.

Throughout this entire period the roles of females as daughters, wives, mothers, and mistresses of homes remained constant. As the prologue confirms, "The profession of ladies, to which the bend of their instruction should be turned, is that of daughters, mothers, and mistresses of families." Yet it is clear—as Thomas Jefferson's letter quoted in chapter four reminds us—that by the early nineteenth century the importance of these roles significantly expanded as mothers became equipped to educate their sons as well as their daughters. Sampler making played a major part in the development of these roles.

NOTES

Chapter One

"To promote the happiness of the little circle"

1. Daniel Blake Smith, "The Study of the Family in Early America: Trends, Problems, and Prospects," p. 18.

2. Gordon S. Wood, *The Radicalism of the American Revolution*, pp. 148–149.

3. For a detailed discussion of changes in the American family, see Steven Mintz and Susan Kellogg, *Domestic Revolutions: A Social History of American Family Life*.

4. Rosealie Stier Calvert, *Mistress of Riverdale: The Plantation Letters of Rosalie Stier Calvert, 1795–1821*, p. 81.

5. Alexis de Tocqueville, April 17, 1819, quoted in Jan Lewis, *The Pursuit of Happiness: Family and Values in Jefferson's Virginia*, p. 158. See Lewis for further elaboration on the definition of happiness.

6. In addition to the verse, the three samplers share large floral borders and water scenes. Of the two samplers not pictured, one is an unsigned sampler, ca. 1828, in the collections of Colonial Williamsburg; the other, by Eliza J. Spratley, also undated, is in a private collection.

7. Jan Lewis has asserted, "It is a commonplace of southern history that the family was of overriding importance, that the family line took precedence over the individual" (*Pursuit of Happiness*, p. 36). This statement seems to be in direct conflict with the establishment of individual rights in what was called the "new American family."

8. Isaac Watts's *Divine Songs for Children* was offered for sale in the *Virginia Almanac* between 1744 and 1765 (information courtesy of John Ingram).

9. Examples of Virginia sampler verses are found in Kimberly A. Smith, "'First Effort of an Infant Hand': An Introduction to Virginia Schoolgirl Embroideries, 1742–1850," pp. 89–98.

10. For example, the following verse has been documented on two other samplers: one from Hanover County, Virginia (in the collections of MESDA), and a second from Liverpool, Nova Scotia (Ethel Stanwood Bolton and Eva Johnson Coe, *American Samplers*, pp. 258, 268):

> When snow descend, and robes the fields
> In winters bright array
> Touched by the sun the lustre fades
> And weeps itself away
>
> When Springs appears—when violets blow
> And shed a rich perfume
> How soon the fragrance breathes its last
> How short lived is the bloom.

11. Bolton and Coe noted, "'*English Notes and Queries* says that this verse was written by the Rev. John Newton for his niece, Miss Elizabeth Catlett. He was at the time Rector of St. Mary's Woolnooth, London'" (*American Samplers*, p. 319).

12. For example, a forty-two page pamphlet entitled "A Sermon, Delivered Jan. 19, 1812, at the Request of a Number of Young Gentlemen of the City of New York, Who Had assembled to Express Their Condolence with the Inhabitants of Richmond, on the Late Mournful Dispensation of Providence in That City" was published by Samuel Miller, pastor of the First Presbyterian Church in the City of New York (items offered for sale August 4, 1955, by Schindler's Antique Shop, Charleston, South Carolina).

13. A broadside in the Valentine Museum collections (*V.50.14*) depicts the theatre but different verses. A second, undated broadside depicts the theatre and poem from which the verses on Sally Clarke Washington's sampler were probably taken (John H. Jenkins, comp., *Early American Imprints: A Collection*

of Works Printed in America between 1669 and 1800, no. 221477). I am indebted to Martha R. Jones for her assistance in the research of this sampler.

14. Stylistically, Anne's sampler is comparable to examples worked at Quaker schools in Burlington County, New Jersey, from the 1820s. Her three-storied house on a mound with animals and men on horseback are similar to motifs found on these Burlington County samplers. Noticeably lacking on Anne's work is the rose and rosebud-vine border consistently found on this group. Perhaps the needlework teacher responsible for her instruction was aware of the Burlington County samplers. See Betty Ring, *Girlhood Embroidery: American Samplers and Pictorial Needlework, 1650–1850*, vol. 2, pp. 476–479.

15. George F. Bragg, *History of the Afro-American Group of the Episcopal Church*, pp. 91–101. The Maryland Historical Society owns a sampler made by Frances Bush at St. James First African P.E. Church in 1832, presumably worked under the guidance of the Reverend Mr. Levington.

16. For a full discussion of Philadelphia presentation samplers, see Ring, *Girlhood Embroidery*, vol. 2, pp. 374–377.

Chapter Two
"My Father Deare Paid for This That I Did Hear"

1. Kathleen Epstein, "Concernynge the Excellency of the Nedle Worcke Spanisshe Stitche," p. 79.

2. Ring, *Girlhood Embroidery*, vol. 1, fig. 1.

3. *Ibid.*, pp. 6–7.

4. Janet Arnold, *Queen Elizabeth's Wardrobe Unlock'd*, p. 190.

5. Averil Colby, *Samplers*, p. 75.

6. See Dorothy Gardiner, *English Girlhood at School: A Study of Women's Education through Twelve Centuries*, for a detailed discussion of the education of English girls at boarding schools during this time period.

7. Ann recorded that she was born "the 8 of Febry AD 1657." Mary listed her birthdate as April 16 of the same year. In addition, Mary stitched the year in which she completed her work, so presumably the two girls finished at about the same time.
I am indebted to Kathleen Epstein for recognizing the similarities in these two samplers.

8. Kathleen Epstein, *An Anonymous Woman: Her Work Wrought in the Seventeenth Century*, p. 13, n. 1.

9. An area of whitework is seen on Elizabeth Cotton's sampler, dated 1698 (fig. 40).

10. Colby, *Samplers*, pp. 116–117.

11. Yet to be fully explored by scholars is the question of why this change occurred. The changing size and shape of samplers may be connected to the finished widths of available ground fabrics. Also, during the eighteenth century the sampler was seen increasingly as an end project worthy of display by the maker's proud parents rather than as a record to be tucked away.

12. Albarta Meulenbelt Nieuwbelt, *Embroidery Motifs from Dutch Samplers*, pp. 149–151.

13. Roger Fiske, *English Theatre Music in the Eighteenth Century*, p. 551.

14. A copperplate-printed cotton in Williamsburg's

collections (*1964-52*) depicts a harlequin figure and beehive.

15. Smith, "'First Effort of an Infant Hand,'" pp. 55, 57.

16. I am indebted to Rebecca Scott for this information. See Joy Jarrett and Rebecca Jarrett Scott, *An A-Z of British Eighteenth- and Nineteenth-Century Samplers*, p. 21.

17. Betty Ring has noted that when American darning samplers are seen, they are usually plain pieces made under Quaker instruction (Betty Ring, *The Joan Stephens Collection: Important Samplers and Pictorial Needlework*, lot 2122).

18. *Instructions on Needlework and Knitting*, p. 18.

19. *Ibid.*, title page.

20. *Ibid.*, p. 5.

21. For further discussion of needlework patterns, see Margaret Swain, *Figures on Fabric: Embroidery Design Sources and Their Application*; Yvonne Hackenbrock, *English and Other Needlework Tapestries and Textiles in the Irwin Untermyer Collection*, pp. xi–liii; and John L. Nevinson, *Catalog of English Domestic Embroidery of the Sixteenth and Seventeenth Centuries*, pp. xxv–xxvi. For patterns in American needlework, see Davida Tenenbaum Deutsch, "Needlework Patterns and Their Use in America," p. 369.

22. In the eighteenth and early nineteenth centuries prints and maps became important sources for needlework designs.

23. Arthur Lotz, *Bibliographie der Modelbücher*, pp. 84–86. I thank Kathleen Epstein for the translation.

24. Unfortunately, Colonial Williamsburg owns no English samplers with designs that have been documented from an early pattern book source.

25. For example, Kathleen Epstein notes in *Anonymous Woman* that drawers working at the Royal Exchange could be hired to draft embroidery patterns (p. 15).

26. Hannah Robertson, *The Young Ladies School of Arts*, p. 27.

27. Pamela Clabburn, *The Needleworker's Dictionary*, p. 56. *Chenille*, the French word for caterpillar, refers to round, furry threads.

28. For a complete discussion of the double running or Spanish stitch see Kathleen Epstein, *A New Modelbook for Spanish Stitch*.

29. Epstein, *Anonymous Woman*, pp. 22–23.

30. Susanna Whatman, *The Housekeeping Book of Susanna Whatman*, p. 45.

31. See chapter 4 for a full discussion of these samplers.

Chapter Three

"There is a Boarding School opened in this town"

1. There is a growing group of identified seventeenth-century American samplers. Loara Standish, of Duxbury, completed the earliest example sometime before 1655 and possibly as early as 1640. Others that have been identified are Mary Atwood, from Plymouth (ca. 1646–1651); Mary Holingworth, from Salem (ca. 1665); Sarah Collins, from Salem (dated 1673); Sarah Stone, from Salem (dated 1678); Elizabeth Cotton of Portsmouth (dated 1698); and Mehitable Payson, from Rowley (ca. 1698–1706). While all but one of these were worked by girls living in what is now Massachusetts (Portsmouth, New Hampshire was part of the Massachusetts Bay Colony in the seventeenth century), recent evidence suggests that sampler making during this time was also practiced in Pennsylvania and New York. (Lecture by Kathleen Epstein, November 1993; and conversation with Kathleen Epstein, April 1997.) Yet to be identified are seventeenth-century Southern samplers.

2. The earliest known Southern sampler, dated July 31, 1729, was worked by Elizabeth Gibbes of Charleston, South Carolina. It is illustrated in Ring, *Girlhood Embroidery*, vol. 2, p. 534, fig. 594.

3. The question of why reversible stitches became outmoded on Northern samplers is still to be fully explored by needlework scholars. This change does not occur in the majority of Virginia samplers until the nineteenth century.

4. See chapter four for a full discussion of the reversibility of patterns seen in some groups of Virginia samplers.

5. Betty Ring, *Let Virtue Be a Guide to Thee: Needlework in the Education of Rhode Island Women, 1730–1830*, pp. 64–67.

6. Susan Burrows Swan, *Plain and Fancy: American Women and Their Needlework, 1650–1850*, pp. 45–50.

7. *Republican*, December 9, 1805.

8. Editorial comment in the newspaper *American Constellation* of 1834, quoted in Suzanne Lebsock, *The Free Women of Petersburg: Status and Culture in a Southern Town, 1784–1860*, p. 64.

9. *Virginia Gazette*, February 27, 1772.

10. *Columbian Mirror and Alexandria Gazette*, July 4, 1795.

11. *Norfolk Herald and Public Advertiser*, September 9, 1797, and *Virginia Argus*, December 6, 1799.

12. For a further discussion of "the first generation of American female educators," see Mary Beth Norton, *Liberty's Daughters: The Revolutionary Experience of American Women, 1750–1800*, pp. 290–294.

13. See, for example, Mary Jaene Edmonds, *Samplers and Samplermakers: An American Schoolgirl Art, 1700–1850*; Glee Krueger, *New England Samplers to 1840*; Ring, *Girlhood Embroidery*, 2 vols.; and Susan Burrows Swan, "Recent Discoveries about Philadelphia Samplers."

14. For a more complete description of samplers and needlework pictures made in the District of Columbia see Ring, *Girlhood Embroidery*, vol. 2, pp. 522–531; and Olive Blair Graffam, "'An Important Branch of Female Education': Needlework in the District of Columbia, 1800–1850," pp. 44–49. Others who have contributed immensely to this area of research are Gloria Seaman Allen and Elisabeth Donaghy Garrett.

15. Thomas Froncek, ed., *An Illustrated History: The City of Washington*, p. 47.

16. *Ibid.*, pp. 138–139.

17. Ring, *Girlhood Embroidery*, vol. 2, p. 530.

18. Sarah Elizabeth Moughon was awarded for her "diligence and attention to her studies" in 1847, possibly the same year she worked a silk-on-silk

bookmark. Both are in the DAR collection. Another certificate, in a private collection, was issued on the same day, February 11, 1847, to Miss Elizabeth Bittinger, who "has been present at the calling of the Roll One Hundred and Twentythree times. . . ."

19. For a similar Philadelphia sampler see Ring, *Joan Stephens Collection*, lot 2089.

20. *Columbian Mirror and Alexandria Gazette*, July 24, 1793. Interestingly in 1794 Mrs. Simson advertised her boarding school in Richmond and in 1795 in Fredericksburg, "where she intends teaching all kinds of Needle-Work in silk and worsted, Darning and Plain Work, in the neatest manner. . . ."

21. Elisabeth Donaghy Garrett, "American Samplers and Needlework Pictures in the DAR Museum, Part II: 1806–1840," pp. 694–695; illus. p. 697.

22. Two of the sampler makers were possibly Catholic, suggesting that the girls were also acquainted with each other through attending the same church.

23. Charlotte Sutherland's 1809 "Washington" sampler is similar in its open ground, format, and variety of stitches. For an illustration see Glee Krueger, *A Gallery of American Samplers: The Theodore H. Kapnek Collection*, p. 47.

24. The maker was initially identified as Julianna Mahala Lawrence, daughter of Colonel John Lawrence and Sarah Shriner of Frederick and Anne Arundel Counties, Maryland. Julianna married her first cousin, Evan Dorsey, Jr. (license November 15, 1828), in Frederick County and moved to Ohio, date unknown. It seems unlikely that at age twenty, two years after her marriage and before moving to Ohio, Julianna would have worked a sampler. It is more probable that another Julianna (or perhaps Tulianna) Lawrence, possibly from the same family, is the maker. See J. D. Warfield, *Founders of Anne Arundel and Howard Counties.*

25. Quoted in Garrett, "American Samplers," pp. 698–700.

26. Froncek, *Illustrated History*, p. 151.

27. *Alexandria Advertiser*, September 28, 1797, and *Norfolk Herald*, July 21, 1796.

28. Gloria Seaman Allen was the curator for the exhibit, *Equally Their Due: Female Education in Antebellum Alexandria*, held at The Lyceum in Alexandria from June 1996 to January 1997.

29. *Alexandria Herald*, September 6, 1820.

30. *Alexandria Daily Gazette*, March 6, 1810.

31. Bolton and Coe, *American Samplers*, pp. 53, 175. Four samplers presumably worked by Ann and Sarah Horwell descended in the family.

32. Bolton and Coe, *American Samplers*, p. 136.

33. In an article to be published in *The Magazine Antiques*, author Gloria Seaman Allen notes that the identity of the school teacher is probably linked to the identity of sampler maker Mary Muir. Incredibly, two Mary Muirs were born at about the same time to Alexandria families associated with female education. In one family the widow Mrs. Muir opened a boarding school for needlework in 1821. In the other Muir family the Reverend James Muir opened a female academy in 1790, which was operated after his death by his wife, Elizabeth, daughters, and the Reverend Elias Harrison. It is possible that the Reverend Mr. Harrison's daughter, Mary, is the Mary Harrison who stitched the 1830 sampler in this group. Scholars are still puzzling over this question.

Chapter Four

"In the neatest manner": Virginia Samplers

1. Wister, Sally, *Sally Wister's Journal: A True Narrative Being a Quaker Maiden's Account of Her Experiences with Officers of the Continental Army*, p. 159.

2. For further discussion on the lack of Southern samplers and needlework, see Heather Ruth Palmer, "Where Is Nineteenth-Century Southern Decorative Needlework?"

3. Calvert, *Mistress of Riversdale*, pp. 85, 188.

4. Philip Fithian's chronicle of his days as tutor to the children of Robert Carter of Nomini Hall in Westmoreland County gives a good account of education on a Virginia plantation in 1773 (Philip Vickers Fithian, *Journal and Letters of Philip Vickers Fithian, 1773–1774: A Plantation Tutor of the Old Dominion*).

5 Ring, *Girlhood Embroidery*, vol. 2, p. 533.

6. *Virginia Gazette*, September 21, 1769, and November 29, 1770.

7. While the number of surviving samplers and needlework pictures worked in Virginia during the colonial period cannot compare at the present time to the numbers from the North, the technical skill seen in Virginia work is exceptional.

8. Anne Blair to Mrs. Mary Braxton, August 21, 1769. Blair, Banister, Braxton, Horner, Whiting Papers, 1765–1890. A tucker is a form of neck kerchief.

9. See fig. 85 for Ann Pasteur Maupin's sampler.

10. Martha Fitzhugh's sampler is in the collection of Arlington House, the Robert E. Lee Memorial, National Park Service. Martha worked her family record sampler in silk cross and eyelet stitches on a linen ground. Measuring 21 in. square, it records the marriage of her parents and births and deaths of siblings. For illustrations of the sampler, see Candace Wheeler, *The Development of Embroidery in America*, facing p. 52; and Gloria Seaman Allen, *Family Record: Genealogical Watercolors and Needlework*, p. 90.

11. Douglas H. Thomas, "Notes and Queries: An Old Sampler," pp. 467–468.

12. Paula B. Ricter, Registrar, Essex Institute, personal communication, July 21, 1989.

13. Norton, *Liberty's Daughters*, pp. 274–276.

14. Thomas Jefferson, *The Jeffersonian Cyclopedia*, vol. 2, p. 274.

15. In this same letter Jefferson instructs Martha to consider her tutor as her own mother (Thomas Jefferson, *Papers of Thomas Jefferson*, vol. 6, pp. 359–360).

16. Thomas Jefferson, *The Family Letters of Thomas Jefferson*, p. 35.

17. *Ibid.*, p. 38.

18. Frances Thacker Burwell's pictorial embroidery is in the collection of the Botetourt County Historical Society, Fincastle, Virginia. It was recorded and photographed by MESDA (Ring, *Girlhood Embroidery*, vol. 2, p. 437).

19. These were Mary Ann Chapman, 1821–1822; Mary Hallam, 1821–1822, 1828; and Harriet Turner Burr, 1829 (Litchfield Historical Society, *To Ornament Their Minds: Sarah Pierce's Litchfield Female Academy, 1792–1833*, pp. 114–131).

20. Listed in *A Brief History of Westtown Boarding School with a General Catalogue of Officers, Students, etc.* I am indebted to Ann Upton for her assistance.

21. For a list of needlework teachers compiled chiefly from newspaper advertisements, see Appendix 2 in Smith, "'First Effort of an Infant Hand.'"

22. In 1736, a thirty-line poem written by "a Gentleman of Virginia To a Lady, On a Screen of her Working" appeared in the *Virginia Gazette* (December 3–10, 1736). It described the needleworker in terms of the flowers stitched on her screen.

23. William D. Hoyt, Jr., "Self Portrait: Eliza Custis, 1808," pp. 97–98.

24. Frances Baylor Hill, "The Diary of Frances Baylor Hill of 'Hillsborough,'" pp. 6, 22–23, 25, 30, 53.

25. This attention to furniture construction techniques includes the use of dust boards, composite block feet, and finished backsides. For further discussion of Virginia furniture, see Wallace B. Gusler, *Furniture of Williamsburg and Eastern Virginia, 1710–1790*; and Ronald L. Hurst and Jonathan Prown, *Southern Furniture 1680–1830: The Colonial Williamsburg Collection*.

26. Mary Johnson did not include her place of residence on her sampler. However, family tradition attributes it to the West Point area, and the birth of a Mary Johnson in 1730 was recorded in the register of St. Peter's Parish, New Kent County. The sampler descended in her family along with a tintype of a later family member (C. G. Chamberlayne, trans. and ed., *The Vestry Book and Register of St. Peter's Parish*, p. 470).

27 The sampler is reported to have been worked by Mary Blaikley Stith, daughter of William and Catharine Blaikley of York County. It records the marriage date of William and Catharine and birth and death dates of their children. Mary Blaikley Stith is buried in Bruton Churchyard in Williamsburg (Lyon G. Tyler, ed., "Notes and Queries," pp. 212–213.

28. William Mead, *Old Churches Ministers and Families of Virginia*, vol. 1, p. 100.

29. Arnold Harris Hord, "Genealogy of the Triplett Family," vol. 21, pp. 118–119; and vol. 22, pp. 310–311.

30. For an extensive discussion of Elizabeth Boush, see Betty Ring, "For Persons of Fortune Who Have Taste: An Elegant Schoolgirl Embroidery," p. 7.

31. *Virginia Gazette*, March 31, 1774.

32. Ring, "For Persons of Fortune," p. 17.

33. Malcolm Hart Harris, compiler, *Old New Kent County: Some Account of the Planters, Plantations, and Places in King William County St. John's Parish*, vol. 2, pp. 636–640; and Georgia Dickinson Wardlaw, *The Old and the Quaint in Virginia*, pp. 10–11.

34. Cornelia Lee's sampler is in the collection of Sully Foundation (*SF51*). Measuring approximately 12 1/2 in. square, it includes this verse: "Ode to Virture / Virtue soft Balm of every Woe / of every [grief] the cure. / tis thou alone that canst best bestow / [Pl]ea[sur]es unmi[xe]d [and] pure."

35. Edmund Jennings Lee, ed., *Lee of Virginia, 1642–1892*, pp. 235, 236, 249–254.

36. *Virginia Gazette*, November 17, 1752.

37. *Ibid.*, December 20, 1776.

38. *Lower Norfolk County Virginia Antiquary*, vol. 1, pt. 1, p. 60; and vol. 2, pt. 1, pp. 24–25.

39. Mary Powell's sampler is in a private collection. It consists of bands of stylized carnations and other flowers, a two-storied building with flanking fruit trees, and a record listing family members' birth dates. The same fruit trees appear on the later Williamsburg group of samplers. A modified version of one of the bands on Mary Powell's embroidery is used as a border on Sarah Walker Waller's sampler. Mary was the daughter of Seymour and Jane Powell of York County. She married Francis Charlton in 1786. Three years later Charles Willson Peale painted a portrait of Mary with her daughter, Jane. Mary died in Williamsburg in 1811.

40. A Virginia bed sheet with the number 2 worked in blue silk is nevertheless embroidered so it is as neat on the back as the front (*1970-36*).

41. Bolton and Coe, *American Samplers*, pp. 53, 332. I would welcome any information on the current location of this sampler.

42. *Enquirer*, November 18, 1808. Another advertisement for a "Williamsburg Ladies Academy" appeared in 1815: "[Y]oung Ladies are Educated by

MR. and MRS. ANDREWS, from Philadelphia in every branch of useful and liberal learning. . . . Drawing, Dancing and Music will be regular'y taught . . . together with the beautiful art of painting on Velvet. . . ." *Norfolk Gazette and Publick Ledger*, October 10, 1815.

43. *Guide to Manuscript Collections of the Colonial Williamsburg Foundation*, no. 134, Miscellaneous Documents, John D. Rockefeller, Jr. Library. I am indebted to Patricia A. Gibbs for bringing this to my attention.

44. Extracts from the records for the Bray School are cited in the training manual *Becoming Americans: Family Story Line*, pp. 222–225.

45. *Norfolk Gazette and Public Ledger*, August 19, 1807. Information courtesy Patricia A. Gibbs.

46. *Brief History of Westtown Boarding School*, pp. 224–295.

47. *Ibid.*, p. 257.

48. Regarding girls being sent away for an education, Mary Beth Norton notes, "The only thing that sustained parents and their daughters through such difficult times was a recognition of the significance of the enterprise upon which they had embarked." For a discussion of this and the change in Americans' attitudes towards female education, see Norton, *Liberty's Daughters*, pp. 275–276.

49. For a similar Westtown sampler with some of the same geometrical half-medallions, see Ann Haines's sampler illustrated in Ring, *Girlhood Embroidery*, vol. 2, p. 392, fig. 427.

50. For further information on the Virginia Quakers, see Jay Worrall, Jr., *The Friendly Virginians: America's First Quakers*, p. 251.

51. William B. Coles, *The Coles Family of Virginia*, pp. 161–162.

52. The fourth sampler, now in a private collection, was worked by Elizabeth Mary Wise (born January 25, 1808), daughter of Tully Rolinson (born July 13, 1784; died December 16, 1825) and Mary Bayne Wise of the Norfolk area. Her large sampler (15 3/8 in. x 25 1/2 in.) is worked in a variety of stitches, including marking cross, on a pieced linen ground. One large band is worked in cross stitch in a triangular pattern to give the appearance of Irish stitch. She also included heart, crown, and star motifs.

53. Accession file, *1978-91*, Department of Collections, Colonial Williamsburg Foundation.

54. Michael E. Pollock, compiler, *Marriage Bonds of Henrico County, Virginia, 1782–1853*, pp. 41, 47. I am indebted to Susan Shames for this reference.

55. For an illustration of the Portsmouth Naval Hospital, see Virginia Historic Landmarks Commission, *The Virginia Landmarks Register: A Profile of the Life and Times of Virginians*, p. 58.

56. Virginia D. Cox and Willie T. Weathers, *Old Houses of King and Queen County, Virginia*, pp. 193–195. I am indebted to Kelly McIntyre for this information. An alternative identification of Wood Lawn School may be the "Woodlawn" in Louisa County, home of William Shelton. In 1813, William Shelton married Maria Coles, maker of the Quaker-style sampler in fig. 94.

57. *Norfolk Herald*, July 21, 1796.

58. Fithian, *Journal and Letters*, p. 42.

59. *Virginia Gazette, or the American Advertiser*, September 4, 1784.

60. For an illustration of a silk embroidery of Palemon and Lavinea from Lititz, Pennsylvania, see Ring, *Girlhood Embroidery*, vol. 2, p. 446, fig. 500.

61. Scottish-born James Thomson was a forerunner of early nineteenth-century romanticism. His work, celebrating nature and an agrarian existence, was extensively used as a subject in American needlework. At least two copies of his book are known to have been in Virginia libraries during this period.

62. Notes from owner.

63. Letter to Barbara R. Luck, Curator, AARFAC,

from Betty Ring, dated August 14, 1989.

64. Accession file, *81.609.3*, AARFAC, Colonial Williamsburg Foundation.

65. Betty Ring, "Needlework Pictures at Bassett Hall," p. 477.

66. For a list of Virginia sampler groups, see App. 1 in Smith, "'First Effort of an Infant Hand.'"

67. Frances Norton Mason, ed., *John Norton and Sons Merchants of London and Virginia: Being the Papers from Their Counting House for the Years 1750 to 1795*, p. 258.

68. Calvert, *Mistress of Riversdale*, p. 101.

69. *Virginia Independent Chronicle*, October 18, 1786.

70. Another group of Richmond-related embroideries consists of samplers made by Mary Calloway White (MESDA, *M3199*), Mildred Malone (Valentine Museum, *V.33,34*), Flora Virginia Holmes (Valentine Museum, *V.36.50.4*) and Amanda A. Bowles. For an illustration of Mary Calloway White's sampler, see Ring, *Girlhood Embroidery*, vol. 2, p. 539, fig. 599. Amanda Bowles's work is pictured in Krueger, *Gallery of American Samplers*, p. 75, fig. 108.

71. Valentine Museum accession records, *V.1898.29.1*, *V.1898.29.2*, and *V.1898.29.3*.

72. *American Beacon and Norfolk and Portsmouth Daily Advertiser*, Virginia, April 29 and December 28, 1820.

73. Almost forty embroideries associated with Loudoun County are illustrated in Betty Whiting Flemming, *Threads of History: A Sampler of Girlhood Embroidery, 1792–1860, Loudoun County Area.*

74. *Lynchburg Press*, September 15, 1814.

75. Susannah S. Rees's sampler is in the collection of the Lynchburg Museum System (*81.35.1*).

76. For an illustration of Catherine Louisa Steele's sampler, see the Carter House, *Tennessee Stitches: An Exhibit of Nineteenth-Century Williamson County Samplers.*

77. R. H. Early, *Campbell Chronicles and Family Sketches Embracing the History of Campbell County, Virginia, 1782–1926*, p. 512.

78. Leading the research in this area is Roddy Moore, a private collector and "Valley of Virginia" scholar.

79. This sampler, in a private collection, depicts an almost identical house with fence and trees. It is marked with the initials AM and AMB and "Rockingham County Virginia 19 December 1845 M."

80. John A. Wayland, *A History of Shenandoah County, Virginia*, pp. 410–413.

81. Two other samplers, in a private collection, are also dated 1844 and are almost identical to Eleanor Hankel's work. The makers are Mary R. Sommers and Elizabeth Shirley.

82. For an illustration of the Henkel home and printery, see Wayland, *History of Shenandoah County*, p. 489.

83. *Ibid.*, pp. 470–471.

84. Martha Wren Briggs, "The Deciphering of Four Stitched Genealogies," pp. 97–113.

85. *American Beacon and Commercial Diary*, December 30, 1816.

86. Hanover County Historical Society, *Old Homes of Hanover County, Virginia*, pp. 14–15; Brown, Coalter, Tucker Papers; Barnes Papers; Rhonda S. Roberson, comp., *1850 Census of King William County.*

87. Information on the insurance of Hill's buildings and a rough sketch of the wooden schoolhouse, which measured 26 ft. x 16 ft., are found in *Mutual Assurance Society of Virginia*, p. 365 (courtesy MESDA research files).

88. *Virginia Argus*, October 21, 1811.

89. Anderson C. Quisenberry, *Memorials of the Quisenberry Family in England, Germany and America*, p. 58. I am indebted to Dywanna M. Saunders for bringing this information to my attention.

90. *Ibid.*, p. 59.

91. Olney Winsor's letters contain frequent refer-

ences to his concern over Nancy's education and about the gratitude that he and his wife should feel to Polly Balch for undertaking their daughter's schooling. In this same letter he writes: "I hope Nancy is not kept so close to working on her Sampler as to injure her Eyes. . . .—you justly observe that is a great piece of work for such a child—therefore great care should be taken to give her proper time of relaxation." Letters of Olney Winsor of Providence, R.I., to his wife, Mrs. Hopec Winsor, written in Alexandria 1786–1788. I am indebted to Ellen K. Donald for this reference.

BIBLIOGRAPHY

Primary Sources

Newspapers

Alexandria Advertiser. Alexandria, Va., 1797.
Alexandria Daily Gazette. Alexandria, Va., 1810.
Alexandria Herald. Alexandria, Va., 1820.
American Beacon and Commercial Diary. Norfolk, Va., 1816.
American Beacon and Norfolk and Portsmouth Daily Advertiser. Norfolk, Va., 1820.
Columbian Mirror and Alexandria Gazette. Alexandria, Va., 1793; 1795.
Enquirer. Richmond, Va., 1808.
Lynchburg Press. Lynchburg, Va., 1814.
Norfolk Gazette and Publick Ledger. Norfolk, Va., 1807; 1815.
Norfolk Herald. Norfolk, Va., 1796.
Norfolk Herald and Public Advertiser. Norfolk, Va., 1797.
Republican. Petersburg, Va., 1805.
Virginia Argus. Richmond, Va., 1799; 1811.
Virginia Gazette. Williamsburg, Va., 1736; 1752; 1766; 1769; 1770; 1772; 1774; 1776.
Virginia Gazette, or the American Advertiser. Richmond, Va., 1784.
Virginia Independent Chronicle. Richmond, Va., 1786.

Virginia Registers

Augusta County Marriage Records, 1813–1845.
Essex County Marriage Register, 1804–1921.
Essex County Register of Births, 1856–1916.
Essex County Register of Deaths, 1856–1916.

Manuscripts and Unpublished Sources

Blair, Banister, Braxton, Horner, Whiting Papers, 1765–1890. Rare Books and Manuscripts, Earl Gregg Swem Library, College of William and Mary, Williamsburg, Va.

Brown, Coalter, Tucker Papers. Rare Books and Manuscripts, Earl Gregg Swem Library, College of William and Mary, Williamsburg, Va.

Barnes Papers. Rare Books and Manuscripts, Earl Gregg Swem Library, College of William and Mary, Williamsburg, Va.

Letters of Olney Winsor of Providence, R.I., to his wife Mrs. Hopec Winsor, written in Alexandria, 1786–1788. Manuscript division, Library of Virginia, Richmond, Va.

Printed Sources

A Brief History of Westtown Boarding School with a General Catalogue of Officers, Students, etc. Philadelphia: Sherman and Co., 1888.

Brown, Margie G., comp. *Genealogical Abstracts: Revolutionary War Veterans Scrip Act, 1852.* Oakton, Va.: published privately, 1990.

Calvert, Rosalie Stier. *Mistress of Riverdale: The Plantation Letters of Rosalie Stier Calvert, 1795–1821.* Ed. Margaret Law Callicott. Baltimore, Md.: John Hopkins University Press, 1991.

Chamberlayne, C. G., trans. and ed. *The Vestry Book and Register of St. Peter's Parish, New Kent and James City Counties, Virginia, 1684–1786.* Richmond, Va.: Virginia State Library, The Library Board, 1937.

Fithian, Philip Vickers. *Journal and Letters of Philip Vickers Fithian, 1773–1774: A Plantation Tutor of the Old Dominion.* Ed. Hunter Dickinson Farish. Charlottesville, Va.: University Press of Virginia, 1968.

Hill, Frances Baylor. "The Diary of Frances Baylor Hill of 'Hillsborough.'" Eds. William K. Bottorff and Roy C. Flannagan. *Early American Literature Newsletter* 2 (winter 1967): 4–53.

Instructions on Needlework and Knitting. London, 1832.

Jefferson, Thomas. *The Family Letters of Thomas Jefferson.* Eds. Edwin Morris Betts and James Adam Bear, Jr. Charlottesville, Va.: University Press of Virginia, 1986.

———. *The Jeffersonian Cyclopedia.* Ed. John P. Foley. Vol. 2. New York: Russell and Russell, 1967.

———. *Papers of Thomas Jefferson.* Eds. Julian Boyd et al. Vol. 6. Princeton, N.J.: Princeton University Press, 1950–1995.

Jenkins, John H., comp. *Early American Imprints: A Collection of Works Printed in America between 1669 and 1800.* 2d series. Austin, Tex.: Jenkins Co., 1977.

Mason, Frances Norton, ed. *John Norton and Sons Merchants of London and Virginia: Being the Papers from their Counting House for the Years 1750 to 1795.* Richmond, Va.: Dietz Press, 1937.

Mutual Assurance Society of Virginia 5 (December 7, 1802).

Roberson, Rhonda S. *1850 Census of King William County.* Norton, Va.: published privately, 198[ ].

Robertson, Hannah. *The Young Ladies School of Arts.* 4th ed. York, Eng., 1777.
Whatman, Susanna. *The Housekeeping Book of Susanna Whatman.* England, 1776.
Williams, Gregory L., and L. Eileen Parrish, eds. *Guide to the Manuscript Collections of the Colonial Williamsburg Foundation.* 3rd ed. Williamsburg, Va.: Colonial Williamsburg Foundation, 1993.
Wister, Sally. *Sally Wister's Journal: A True Narrative Being a Quaker Maiden's Account of Her Experiences with Officers of the Continental Army, 1777–1778.* Ed. Albert Cook Myers. Philadelphia: Ferris and Leach, 1902.

Secondary Sources

Adler, Susan. "Anne Maria Clarke's Sampler: A Technical and Historical Examination." Manuscript, Valentine Museum, Richmond, Va.
Allen, Gloria Seaman. *Family Record: Genealogical Watercolors and Needlework.* Washington, D.C.: DAR Museum, 1989. Exhibit catalog.
———. "Needlework Education in Antebellum Alexandria." *The Magazine Antiques.* Forthcoming.
Arnold, Janet. *Queen Elizabeth's Wardrobe Unlock'd.* Leeds, Great Britain: W. S. Maney and Son, 1988.
Barrett, Mrs. Russel S. "Marriage Bonds of Norfolk County." *William and Mary Quarterly* 8, no. 2 (1928): 99–110.
Bolton, Ethel Stanwood, and Eva Johnston Coe. *American Samplers.* Boston: Society of the Colonial Dames of America, 1921.
Bowen, Helen. "The Fishing Lady and the Boston Common." *The Magazine Antiques* 4, no. 2 (1923): 70–73.
Bragg, George F. *History of the Afro-American Group of the Episcopal Church.* Baltimore, Md.: Church Advocate Press, 1922.
Briggs, Martha Wren. "The Deciphering of Four Stitched Genealogies." *Virginia Tidewater Genealogy* 20, no. 3 (1989): 97–113.
Cabot, Nancy Graves. "The Fishing Lady and the Boston Common." *The Magazine Antiques* 40, no. 1 (1941): 28–31.
———. "Engravings and Embroideries: The Sources of Some Designs in the Fishing Lady Pictures." *The Magazine Antiques* 40, no. 6 (1941): 367–369.
Early, R. H. *Campbell Chronicles and Family Sketches Embracing the History of Campbell County, Virginia, 1782–1926.* Lynchburg, Va.: J. P. Bell, 1927.
Carter House. *Tennessee Stitches: An Exhibit of Nineteenth-Century Williamson County Samplers.* Franklin, Tenn.: Carter House, 1993. Exhibit catalog.
Clabburn, Pamela. *The Needleworker's Dictionary.* London: Macmillan, 1976.
Colby, Averil. *Samplers.* London: B. T. Batsford, 1964.
Coles, William B. *The Coles Family of Virginia.* Baltimore, Md.: Gateway Press, 1989.
Colonial Williamsburg Foundation. *Becoming Americans: Family Story Line.* December 1996. Employee training manual.
Cowles, Calvin Duvall, comp. *Genealogy of the Cowles Families in America.* Vol. 1. New Haven, Conn.: Tuttle, Morehouse and Taylor, 1929.
Cox, Virginia D., and Willie T. Weathers. *Old Houses of King and Queen County, Virginia.* Richmond, Va.: King and Queen County Historical Society, 1973.
Deutsch, Davida Tenenbaum. "Needlework Patterns and Their Use in America." *The Magazine Antiques* 139, no. 2 (1991): 368–381.
Edmonds, Mary Jaene. *Samplers and Samplermakers: An American Schoolgirl Art, 1700–1850.* New York: Rizzoli, 1991.
Epstein, Kathleen A. *An Anonymous Woman: Her Work Wrought in the Seventeenth Century.* Austin, Tex.: Curious Works Press, 1992.
———. *A New Modelbook for Spanish Stitch.* Austin, Tex.: Curious Works Press, 1993.
———. "Concernynge the Excellency of the Nedle Worcke Spanisshe Stitche." *Piecework Magazine* 3, no. 1 (1995): 73–83.
European and American Furniture and Decorative Arts and Silver. San Francisco: Butterfield and Butterfield, Auctioneers, 1997. Auction catalog.
Finkel, Amy, and Morris Finkel. *Samplers: A Selected Offering of Antique Samplers and Needlework* 10. Philadelphia: published privately, 1996. Sales catalog.
Fiske, Roger. *English Theatre Music in the Eighteenth Century.* Oxford: Oxford University Press, 1986.
Flemming, Betty Whiting. *Threads of History: A Sampler of Girlhood Embroidery, 1792–1860, Loudoun County Area.* Leesburg, Va.: Loudoun Museum, 1995.
Froncek, Thomas, ed. *An Illustrated History: The City of Washington.* New York: Alfred A. Knopf, 1997.
Gardiner, Dorothy. *English Girlhood at School: A Study of Women's Education through Twelve Centuries.* Oxford: Oxford University Press, 1929.

Garrett, Elisabeth Donaghy. "American Samplers and Needlework Pictures in the DAR Museum, Part II: 1806–1840." *The Magazine Antiques* 107, no. 4 (1975): 688–701.

———. "Canterbury Tales: Notes on a New Hampshire School of Needlework." In *Lessons Stitched in Silk: Samplers from the Canterbury Region of New Hampshire*. Dartmouth, N.H.: Hood Museum of Art, 1990. Exhibit catalog.

Graffam, Olive Blair. " 'An Important Branch of Female Education': Needlework in the District of Columbia, 1800–1850." In *Historic Alexandria Antique Show*. 1994. Show catalog.

Gusler, Wallace B. *Furniture of Williamsburg and Eastern Virginia*. Reprint. Williamsburg, Va.: Colonial Williamsburg Foundation, 1993.

Hackenbrock, Yvonne. *English and Other Needlework Tapestries and Textiles in the Irwin Untermyer Collection*. Cambridge, Mass.: Harvard University Press, 1960.

Hanover County Historical Society. *Old Homes of Hanover County, Virginia*. Hanover, Va.: Hanover County Historical Society, 1983.

Harris, Malcolm Hart, comp. *Old New Kent County: Some Account of the Planters, Plantations, and Places in King William County St. John's Parish*. Vol. 2. West Point, Va.: published privately, 1977.

Hayden, Horace Edwin. *Virginia Genealogies: A Genealogy of the Glassell Family of Scotland and Virginia*. Baltimore, Md.: Genealogical Publishing, 1979.

Hersh, Tandy, and Charles Hersh. *Samplers of the Pennsylvania Germans*. Birdsboro, Pa.: Pennsylvania German Society, 1991.

Hord, Arnold Harris. "Genealogy of the Triplett Family." Pts. 1 and 2. *William and Mary College Quarterly* 21, no. 2 (1912): 115–134; 22, no. 3 (1914): 175–181.

Howland, Franklyn. *A Brief Genealogical and Biographical History of Arthur Henry, and John Howland and Their Descendants, of the United States and Canada*. Ann Arbor, Mich.: University Microfilm, 1991.

Hoyt, William D., Jr. "Self Portrait: Eliza Custis, 1808." *Virginia Magazine of History and Biography* 53, no. 2 (1945): 89–100.

Hurst, Ronald L., and Jonathan Prown. *Southern Furniture 1680–1830: The Colonial Williamsburg Collection*. Williamsburg, Va.: Colonial Williamsburg Foundation; New York: Harry N. Abrams, 1997.

Important Americana. Sotheby's Auction Catalog, October 22, 1995.

Jarrett, Joy, and Rebecca Jarrett Scott. *An A-Z of British Eighteenth- and Nineteenth-Century Samplers*. Witney, Eng.: published privately, 1993.

Krueger, Glee. *A Gallery of American Samplers: The Theodore H. Kapnek Collection*. New York: Bonanza Books, 1978.

———. *New England Samplers to 1840*. Sturbridge, Mass.: Old Sturbridge Village, 1978.

LaBranche, John F., and Rita F. Conant. *In Female Worth and Elegance: Sampler and Needlework Students and Teachers in Portsmouth, New Hampshire, 1741–1840*. Portsmouth, N.H.: Peter E. Randall, 1996.

Lebsock, Suzanne. *The Free Women of Petersburg: Status and Culture in a Southern Town, 1784–1860*. New York: Norton, 1984.

Lee, Edmund Jennings, ed. *Lee of Virginia, 1642–1892: Biographical and Genealogical Sketches of the Descendants of Colonel Richard Lee*. Baltimore, Md.: Genealogical Publishing, 1983.

Lewis, Jan. *The Pursuit of Happiness: Family and Values in Jefferson's Virginia*. New York: Cambridge University Press, 1983.

Lower Norfolk County Virginia Antiquary. Vol. 1, 1895; vol. 2, 1897.

Litchfield Historical Society. *To Ornament Their Minds: Sarah Pierce's Litchfield Female Academy, 1792–1833*. Litchfield, Conn.: Litchfield Historical Society, 1993.

Lotz, Arthur. *Bibliographie der Modelbücher*. Stuttgart: Anton Hiersemann, 1963.

Lutz, Frances Earle. *Chesterfield, an Old Virginia County*. Richmond, Va.: W. Byrd Press, 1954.

Mackenzie, George Norbury, and Nelson Osgood Rhodes. *Colonial Families of the United States*. New York: Grafton Press, 1907.

Meade, William. *Old Churches, Ministers, and Families of Virginia*. Comp. Jennings Cropper Wise. Vol. 1. Baltimore, Md.: Genealogical Publishing, 1966 [1857].

Mintz, Steven, and Susan Kellogg. *Domestic Revolutions: A Social History of American Family Life*. New York: Free Press, 1988.

Mitchell, Theodore, and Heather Caldwell. "Through the Eye of the Needle: The Education of Women in Canterbury, New Hampshire, 1780–1840." In *Lessons Stitched in Silk: Samplers from the Canterbury Region of New Hampshire*. Dartmouth, N.H.: Hood Museum of Art, 1990. Exhibit catalog.

Nevinson, John L. *Catalog of English Domestic Embroidery of the Sixteenth and Seventeenth Centuries*. London: His Majesty's Stationery Office, 1950.

Nieuwbelt, Albarta Meulenbelt. *Embroidery Motifs from Dutch Samplers.* London: B. T. Batsford, 1974.
Norton, Mary Beth. *Liberty's Daughters: The Revolutionary Experience of American Women, 1750–1800.* Boston: Little, Brown, 1980.
Noyes, Sybil, Charles Thornton Libby, and Walter Goodwin Davis. *Genealogical Dictionary of Maine and New Hampshire.* Portland, Ore.: Southworth-Anthoensen Press, 1928.
Palmer, Heather Ruth. "Where Is Nineteenth-Century Southern Decorative Needlework?" *The Southern Quarterly* 27, no. 1 (1988): 57–71.
Page, Richard C. M. *Genealogy of the Page Family in Virginia.* Harrisonburg, Va.: C. J. Carrier, 1972.
Pollock, Michael, comp. *Marriage Bonds of Henrico County, Virginia, 1782–1853.* Baltimore, Md.: Genealogical Publishing, 1984.
Quisenberry, Anderson C. *Memorials of the Quisenberry Family in England, Germany and America.* Washington, D.C.: Gibson Bros., 1900.
Ring, Betty. "For Persons of Fortune Who Have Taste: An Elegant Schoolgirl Embroidery." *Journal of Early Southern Decorative Arts* 3, no. 2 (1977): 1–23.
———. "Needlework Pictures at Bassett Hall." *The Magazine Antiques* 121, no. 2 (1982): 476–482.
———. *Let Virtue Be a Guide to Thee: Needlework in the Education of Rhode Island Women, 1730–1830.* Providence, R.I.: The Rhode Island Historical Society, 1983.
———. *Girlhood Embroidery: American Samplers and Pictorial Needlework 1650–1850.* 2 vols. New York: Alfred A. Knopf, 1993.
———. *The Joan Stephens Collection: Important Samplers and Pictorial Needlework.* New York: Sotheby's, January 19, 1997. Auction catalog.
Smith, Daniel Blake. "The Study of the Family in Early America: Trends, Problems, and Prospects." *The William and Mary Quarterly* 39, no. 1 (1982): 3–28.
Smith, Kimberly A. "'First Effort of an Infant Hand': An Introduction to Virginia Schoolgirl Embroideries, 1742–1850." *Journal of Early Southern Decorative Arts* 16, no. 2 (1990): 31–101.
Swain, Margaret. *Figures on Fabric: Embroidery Design Sources and Their Application.* London: Adam and Charles Black, 1980.
Swan, Susan Burrows. "Recent Discoveries about Philadelphia Samplers." *The Magazine Antiques* 136, no. 6 (1989): 1334–1343.
———. *Plain and Fancy: American Women and Their Needlework, 1650–1850.* Rev. ed. Austin, Tex.: Curious Works Press, 1995.
Thomas, Douglas H. "Notes and Queries: An Old Sampler." *Virginia Magazine of History and Biography* 4, no. 4 (1897): 467–468.
"Travis Family." *William and Mary Quarterly* 18, no. 2 (1909): 141–144.
Tyler, Lyon G. "Notes and Queries." *William and Mary Quarterly* 2, no. 3 (1894): 212–213.
Virginia Historic Landmarks Commission. *The Virginia Landmarks Register: A Profile of the Life and Times of Virginians.* Richmond, Va.: Virginia Historic Landmarks Commission, 1976.
Wardlaw, Georgia Dickinson. *The Old and the Quaint in Virginia.* Richmond, Va.: Dietz Press, 1939.
Warfield, J. D. *Founders of Anne Arundel and Howard Counties.* Baltimore, Md.: Regional Publishing, 1980.
Wayland, John A. *A History of Shenandoah County, Virginia.* Strasburg, Va.: Shenandoah Publishing House, 1969.
Weisiger, Benjamin. *Chesterfield County, Virginia Deeds 1756–64.* Richmond, Va.: published privately, 1989.
Wheeler, Candace. *The Development of Embroidery in America.* New York: Harper and Brothers, 1921.
Wood, Gordon S. *The Radicalism of the American Revolution.* New York: Alfred A. Knopf, 1992.
Worrall, Jay Jr. *The Friendly Virginians: America's First Quakers.* Athens, Ga.: Iberian Publishing, 1994.

INDEX

References to illustrations are printed in italic type.